A Miscellany

Edward Thomas
A Miscellany

Introduction and selection
by Anna Stenning

Rucksack Editions

Galileo Publishers, Cambridge

Published by Galileo Publishers
16 Woodlands Road, Great Shelford,
Cambridge, UK, CB22 5LW

www.galileopublishing.co.uk

Galileo Publishers is an imprint of
Galileo Multimedia Ltd.

ISBN 978-1-903385-60-9

Text design by James Shurmer

Cover design by NamdesignUK

Cover illustration by Paul Nash

Rucksack Editions are based on an original concept by
Erlend Clouston

Printed in Lithuania

Also in the series:

Contents

Introduction by Anna Stenning

Edward Thomas is best known as a poet of the First World War: he was killed in the Battle of Arras in 1917. However he had spent most of his life as a walker, a naturalist, a countryside writer and a literary critic with a passion for the countryside, and if his earlier work is known, it may be mistakenly relegated to what is now a distant past – a world where footpaths went on forever, and endless summer days full of bird song were followed by dark and starry nights. Indeed, Thomas may sometimes have written as though winters would always be snowy, and the wanderer could take refuge by the firesides of friendly country inns. But the truth is that during the course of Thomas's life between 1878 and 1917, the traditional life of the countryside had altered drastically. Even if that had not been the case, a middle-class Londoner like Thomas would not have belonged to the rural social order. He wrote about villages, inns, wildlife and folk music from the perspective of an enthusiastic outsider. Like his friends and contemporaries Thomas Hardy, John Masefield, Arthur Ransome and Walter de la Mare, Thomas had to piece together how to appreciate the 'joy of the open air' from fragments: from people he met and read, and from his childhood memories. Fortunately Thomas was a gifted traveller along both the literal road and the metaphorical journey of discovery into this landscape.

Thomas's specialities were walking (some friends called him 'Walking Tom') together with his use of keen eyes and ears, and through these he offered the modern rambler or walker a way to 'read' the landscape for its history, wildlife and emotional impact. He noticed the decline in buzzard populations through game-keeping practices, the changing seasonal patterns of plants, the impact of industry, car use, suburban homes and tourists, as well as the longer-scale developments of human settlements, labour and language. At the same time he sought out activities that had been carried out for many centuries such as haymaking, brewing, horticulture, and dairying. We can benefit from Thomas's observational skills and enjoy his vivid experiences of springtime flowers, birdsong and folk music from the last era before the mechanisation of agriculture changed the English countryside for ever. And just as in his own process of 're-discovery' he was aware of the rhythms of seasons and decades, so too was he able to capture specific moments, through his lyric poetry and prose sketches.

The keen eye which Thomas needed as a 'forward-observer' for the Royal Garrison Artillery during the Great War came from walking the ancient paths of the English and Welsh countryside, looking for the first spring violets with his children. The knowledge of birds, plants and trees which he had developed from early childhood meant he could spot things that no one else noticed, from rare birds and their nests to the then everyday species that he thought were the most beautiful – lesser celandines and wild primroses, blackbirds and thrushes. He saw how the 'peculiar combination of soil and water and woodland' produced ancient trackways and settlements; sought to learn 'folk-lore, legends, place-names' so that we might give 'life to past times'.[1]

For Thomas, walking ancient footpaths and old roads created an imaginative connection with the landscape and constituted a kind of early 'psycho-geography'. He never wrote a traditional guide book (he claimed he had no 'social sense'), but he described in compelling detail both the newest developments and those which were already well under way – the progressive decline in demand for rural labour, for instance – and he recorded their emotional as much as their economic impact. He knew there was no going back, and no point writing 'as if there were no such thing as a Tube, Grape Nuts, Love of Nature, a Fabian Society, A Bill for the Reform of Marriage Laws'.[2] But his writing suggests that in spite of (or perhaps more accurately, because of) modern technology, direct experiences of nature and the countryside were all the more important.

In his book about the southern English countryside, Thomas said he had written about something 'far smaller' than the actual landscape, 'as when a mountain with tracts of sky and cloud and the full moon glass them in a pond, a little pond'.[3] He underplayed his intellectual achievements, which included a deep knowledge of British and European literature (he was a leading literary critic in the lead-up to the First World War), and he criticised himself relentlessly for what he saw as his shortcomings. He was a contradictory man: he suffered from depression, but he was full of jokes and had many friends; he studied history at Oxford, but didn't like historical tourism; he thought of himself as mainly Welsh, but dedicated his life to English literature. And perhaps the greatest contradiction was that he was unable to return the devotion of his wife, for whom he nevertheless and undoubtedly cared deeply. He depended absolutely on the inspirational power of literature, and spent his life recording the minutia of unfolding experience. He noticed the irreconcilable strangeness of birds feasting on thistles in a 'hollow wood'; a child's all-consuming experience of beauty; the umbrella salesman's disappointing Sunday meal; the dead soldier-ploughman's abandoned work; the hermits, tramps, misfits, and poets; the surprising lives of roadside verges, hedgerows and chalk pits. It is ironic that a man who was plagued by depression can so inspire us to appreciate the wonderful details and contingencies of existence.

Edward Thomas was born in March 1878 in London. His Welsh parents had left South Wales a generation earlier to find work. His paternal grandfather was a fitter for the Great Western Railway in Swindon before his father, Philip Thomas, became a staff clerk at the Board of Trade. As a child on holiday in Wiltshire, Edward Thomas became friends with a man called 'Dad' Uzzel, a farm worker who inspired Thomas's love of the countryside, and visits to his Welsh family ignited his passion for the country and its Bardic tradition. At home in South London, and influenced by the Victorian country writer Richard Jefferies, Thomas sought nature on the edge of the city, and started writing about his experiences from an early age. Edward was the eldest of six brothers, and while he adored his mother, he struggled to live up to his father's expectations of upward mobility. Although the young Edward was painfully shy, he was encouraged, initially by his family's minister, and later by a local man called James Ashcroft Noble, to become a professional writer. Edward started a young, but all consuming, relationship with Noble's daughter, Helen. She became his wife and they had three children together — the first while Thomas was still at university.

During his career, Thomas compiled a number of anthologies on nature, literature and poetry. One of them, *A Pocket Book of Poems and Songs For the Open Air*, from 1907, included poems from his friends and contemporaries, as well as folk songs chosen for the pleasure it was hoped they would give. The selection of Thomas's poems and prose in this volume has been chosen to serve the same purpose. It includes practical observations as well as literary asides, and it introduces Thomas as a companion to reassess the English and Welsh countryside. To his family, to his many friends and to his contemporary readers, Thomas was a faithful and inspirational guide to the wild places of England and Wales. As this *Miscellany* shows, he remains a wise and amiable walking companion.

NOTES AND REFERENCES

1   Edward Thomas, *The South Country* (1909), 147.
2   Edward Thomas, review of Wilfrid Gibson's *The Nets of Love* in 1905.
3   Thomas, *The South Country*, 10.

Chapter One

Birds

Edward Thomas's countryside writing, diaries, fiction for children and adults, and poetry abounds with birds. In his non-fiction Edward Thomas recorded the behaviour of birds in different seasons, habitats and weathers, with the eye and ear of the ornithologist and a preference for walking in secluded, unpeopled places. Thomas's passion for birds started early. In the stories, poems, essays and countryside books, he walked in the steps of the poets who saw birds as a metaphor for our own lives; yet he wrote with the naturalist's awareness of particular species. This is why encounters with everyday birds were so important to him (he was more of a birder than a 'twitcher'). He showed that birds and birdsong give us rare moments of pleasure and attentiveness in an otherwise frantic world. More than that, his writing explained why we should care for the loss of individual species.

Thomas's first book, *The Woodland Life*, includes essays on a Wiltshire poacher, Richmond Park and 'A Pinewood near London'. It describes the everyday life of the countryside through the seasons, and it features a naturalist's diary with detailed botanical records. These observations contribute to a picture of how the environment has changed in the past 100 years, particularly the differences in urban and farm wildlife. Even in Thomas's day, however, urban expansion threatened the neighbouring countryside.

While Thomas did not write any complete poems during his time in the trenches, he kept a private diary in his last three months as a soldier, as he often had throughout his life, and part of this is also reproduced here.

Apart from travel books, countryside writing, essays, reviews, literary criticism and biographies, Thomas also wrote fiction. 'The Friend of the Blackbird' is a story from his posthumously published collection of journalism and stories entitled *The Last Sheaf*. Thomas's *Four-and-Twenty Blackbirds* is his only collection of stories for children. Originating in stories written for his children, Myfanwy, Merfyn and Bronwen, Thomas finished the collection with the help of his friend Eleanor Farjeon, who was just beginning her own career as a writer.[4]

March 3rd was Edward Thomas's birthday. Edna Longley links the poem by the same name to the chiffchaff's song, which Thomas described as the herald of spring in *In Pursuit of Spring* and *The South Country*.[5] Robert Frost used *In Pursuit of Spring* (1914) to convince Thomas that he had the skills to be a poet, and the book was a source for some of Thomas's later poems. So the chiffchaff becomes, in more ways than one, a symbol of Thomas's imaginative awakening.

The Countryside – 'The Extinction of a Bird'

For some the country is hardly more than an alternative to theatres, exhibitions, clubs, or pills. A large number find in a country mixture of sport, natural history, archaeology, and vagabondage, in the society of the lonely sea, what most calls out and contents their deeper genial instincts: on the hills or in forests they do not feel themselves to be mere spirits fettered to restless but heavy bodies, or mere bodies with starving spirits, but can, for 'moments big as years' and even for some weeks, feel only a little lower than the animals as well as the angels.[6] The country gives them more encouragement to moods of ease and a sense of unity with life, more obvious opportunities than the town for self-reliance and freedom from the confounding para phernalia of civilization. Other men, like that Italian of the Renaissance, have shed tears at the sight of noble trees and waving cornfields, and a long landscape has cured their sickness.[7] To these and some others the country is the principal reality outside themselves: there only are they at home, and the city seems to them an accident, perhaps an unnecessary one. They do not care the less for individual men, they are not indifferent to movements affecting multitudes, they may even have become entangled in one or another kind of social net, but they recognize only two great things, Nature and the heart of man. The extinction of a bird may rouse them, as it has done the poet, Mr. Ralph Hodgson, to sorrow both for the loss of beauty and for the wound given to an ancient order which passes man's understanding.[8] (*The Country*, 1913, 37–8)

1. Pewits (or Lapwings; *Vanellus vanellus*) – Winter Fields

At length the road emerges from its groove on to the hilltop, and once more it is level and bounded by narrow woods of spruce, whence comes the startling challenge of the pheasant-cocks. Meanwhile the twilight air has become keener and the wind rises – humming through the green firs. The smaller birds are nearly all in cover, and only a belated pipit or a steady flapping rook moves aloft in the rude air. Sometimes, in the hedges that line the way, robins rustle gently and fly a yard or two, or a blackbird blusters out; otherwise the life so lately stirring is silent, and the tomtits are rocked asleep amid the swaying larch-boughs.

Out in the fields, freshly turned by the plough, peewits [pewits] run rapidly hither and thither, occasionally chirruping a low distressful note, unlike their usual screaming wail. The whole flock is within thirty yards of us, and their markings are perfectly clear, – the flowing crest, the dark band beneath the throat, and the snow-white breast, showing against the clods. With the chilling wind the snow begins to fall again, and from the shelter of this holly-tree we can watch the flakes drifting swiftly across the meadows, and rolling like thin smoke, silvering the sward and heaping by the ditches. Still the peewits move uneasily in the open, always facing the wind and the thin wall of snow bearing down upon them. Scared by a sportsman passing near them, several rise, but soon settle again, running a short distance in the very teeth of the blast. Some of them stand huddled in the furrows, as partridges do by the ant-hillocks. At length the snow ceases and the wind drops to a whisper; then over the hilltop the lapwings start up again and wheel in phantom flight, shrieking their weird night call. (From 'A Touch of Winter', *The Woodland Life*, 1897, 115–17)

'Two Pewits' (May 1915, *Poems*)

> Under the after-sunset sky
> Two pewits sport and cry,
> More white than is the moon on high
> Riding the dark surge silently;
> More black than earth. Their cry
> Is the one sound under the sky.
> They alone move, now low, now high,
> And merrily they cry
> To the mischievous Spring sky,

Plunging earthward, tossing high,
Over the ghost who wonders why
So merrily they cry and fly,
Nor choose 'twixt earth and sky,
While the moon's quarter silently
Rides, and earth rests as silently.

Blackbirds – 'The Friend of the Blackbird'

For the whole of one year, whenever my daily walks led me down a certain old lane that used to be full of sun and forgetfulness, I was sure not to have it to myself. It was no longer used as a road, the farm it had served once being covered up in ivy and nettle; and as a footpath it was not a short cut to anywhere. Until that year I had met no one there. I have not met anyone there since. He was nearly always in the same place, just where the first bend in the lane shut out the road. At first, I thought he looked unusually out of place, with his new, stiff clothes, tall grey hat, polished ebony walking-stick, and movements angular and precise. I was not glad to see him – an invalid, I supposed – in a place which I once believed my own, and could not regard as a thoroughfare.

One day he stopped me by asking the name of a flower which he pointed out tenderly and politely with his glossy stick. As he spoke he turned his eyes towards me, though hardly upon me, so that I seemed to be bathed in their light, which had a cold brightness and purity as of newly melted frost, and a blissfulness also which was so intense as to be unearthly. Clearly he was one who saw invisible things. Feeling that he was not looking at me I could observe his eyes closely, and they were indifferent to my curiosity. They were moistly bright, of a clear grey, and almost circular, the lids being unnoticeable under the gentle arches of thick, light-brown eyebrows; their expression was of childlike earnestness and simplicity, tinged with surprise that might almost have been fear. His face was square, and the delicate skin, drawn tightly over prominent bones, was nearly all concealed by the short brown hair on cheeks, lips and chin. Through the hair showed a pair of lips matching the eyes — full, moist, shapely and soft, of an unblemished innocence. He was short, squarely but lightly made. His voice was in keeping with his eyes and lips; it was deep, slow, and soft almost to a breaking point.

I saw him many times before we spoke more than a few words again. As I passed he used to cast upon me that bright, unchanging glance without any kindliness in its gentleness, and seemed to feel rather than to see that I was on that common plane where everybody knows what you mean because you mean nothing in particular. In reply I could only look upon him with curiosity that was quickly overcome with discomfort, by awe, and even a kind of dread. Beauty, genius, or happiness, each in its own way, compels awe akin to fear, in the detached beholder. This man had happiness. Never before or since have I seen happiness so shining. Where at first I had blindly seen his external incongruity with the untended hawthorns and virgin grass, I came to see perfect fitness. He was entirely at home there. In my memory the intensity of his happiness is all the more wondrous because of the pain of his end not much more than a year after I saw him first.

He knew himself that he was to die soon.

He was the son of a farmer among the mountains. When he had to go to school at eight or nine years old, it was in a town within sight of the ridges, but thirty miles away. In the town he had grown up. He was there when his father died, and except on the day of the funeral he never revisited home. Tired of school, he left of his own accord and became a collier. For six days out of seven he washed only his lips clean, and that with ale. At the end of the sixth he washed his whole face, that he might kiss a maid. He fell in love. But the maid died, and at her funeral he dropped, fainting, into the grave. From that day he began to read all night. He seldom saw the sun, except on Sundays, and then only through the windows of his bedroom where he worked, or of his chapel. He began to preach, and in a few years was thought fit to be a minister. His furious pieties in the pulpit won him at first a congregation that would travel many mountain leagues on horseback or foot to hear him. But out of the pulpit he was a different man. He was silent and morose. He would take no part in festivals, in music, in politics, in judgements of erring man or woman. They thought him proud; they muttered that they would not go on paying a man to mount up into the clouds for one day in the week, and when he had recovered from a long illness, he found he must go to a small house in the hills to serve two chapels many miles apart. He had loved God over-much. But he did not cease from loving. God hid Himself from this worshipper, but he kneeled and smiled as if God had loved him. He thought of no one else; there was none but Him and of Him he thought as winter changed to spring and spring to summer, and summer to winter, as roads glide into one another. He did not look down to behold the earth and sea, nor up to the sky. There was nothing for him but God, and the two little grey chapels far from man, on the great moors.

Once again he fell ill and in his delirium the truth passed before his eyes – that he had loved God overmuch and His creatures too little. Sickness left him unable to walk any more from chapel to chapel over the cloudy hills. He had to teach little children in a hamlet so poor they were glad of him. There he lived alone, except for the children and the birds that inhabit the lean oaks of the stony copses, the alders along the brooks, the fern upon the lone crag that filled half of his northern sky. Since his illness he had forgotten about God, and remembered only the misery of his creatures. But the children and the birds cheered and taught him. On this earth he learned that it was a man's part to love the earth and its children. There would be plenty of time left in eternity for loving God. We do not demand, he reflected, that the maidservant lighting a fire at dawn should think about the sun, or that the soldier loading his rifle should think about his king; and so an earthly man need not greatly be troubled about anything but his fellow-men and animals, companions of the brief lifetime that is as a meadow in one of the folds in the mountain of eternity. In those old days, he thought, when the Lord went over Jordan with the children of Israel, men were as children, and He walked with them, but now He has ascended and we see Him not until we also shall have gone up, we know not whither. Nor did his thought perish when another sickness overthrew him and left him one hand trembling as if it were no longer his own. The children presented him with the ebony stick, and he left them to die. In the meantime he had taken to this lane.

Sometimes he brought a book out with him, and when he did, it was a book of travel or natural history. He had an inexhaustible desire to know about everything that lives on earth, both near and far. He had learned the songs of many birds, and spoke of them familiarly and with delight. The immensity and variety of Nature, as he found himself, or read of in the gorgeous records of travellers, were a source of continual satisfaction; he had never dreamed of them before. Everywhere he found beauty, personality, and differences without end. The old simplicity and horror of the world conceived as the abode of evil man and dissatisfied, incompatible Deity were forgotten. He could speak of God without emotion. After reading a book in which a liberal and gentle soul created a liberal and gentle Deity, and showed the necessity of his own adherence to the religion of his fathers, his only comment was: 'It was a good book … a good God, but not a very great God after all … what does that thrush say? We must consider him. But so far they do not seem to know very much about him, except his skeleton and his diet. There must be one God for both of us. We can afford to wait. So can He'. But that was only a casual, light-hearted expression of the creed that was coming to him under the sky. He turned away to look at a blackcap singing every minute high up in golden-green blossom against the blue sky, where the sun and the southwest wind ruled over large, eager clouds with edges of gleaming white. The little dead-leaf coloured bird quivered all over; his throat swelled in bubble after bubble; his lifted black head was turned from side to side as he sang; and he moved slowly among the blossom.

The high, quick, dewy notes filled the paralytic with a thin, exquisite pleasure, as if his soul had climbed upon the line of his vision and crept into the singing bird. 'All these things are not mine. They are me. And that is not all: I am them. We are one. We are organs and instruments of one another.' He did not forget the trees – 'those tethered dreamers, standing on one leg like Indian mystics.' With them also he felt the same community, as though more rarely and in a way not to be spoken except by putting out his hand to touch their bark and leaves. The animals, too, were more remote than the birds, and reminded him too often of men's careless sins of cruelty. He did not preach kindness to animals, but pitied those men who had not yet awakened to the need of kindness, as if they must be suffering for the lack as much as the animals. He could not tell why men kept birds in cages to sing. Their freedom in living and dying was lovely to him. Every creature, including man, is best in freedom, he said, looking up at the white clouds coursing in the freedom that was from everlasting to everlasting. He sighed with regret, mingled with apology, as animals slipped away out of sight. Then he was glad to hear the blackbird and thrush again, the sweet, lively talking of the thrush and the pure melody of the blackbird. They were his favourites. He could talk of the different blackbirds he had known, and their places in town or wild, and describe their differences. With a little laugh, because he remembered the days before he had such thoughts, he said plainly that they had souls and lived, as we do, after death, though he did not know, nor perhaps did they, what life it might be. Only, there was one thing in the blackbird that he could not enjoy – probably, he admitted, because he could not understand; and that was the laughing, discordant notes that often concluded his song, especially in the late spring. This distressed him, partly because it was not musically in keeping with the song, and partly because the bird seemed to be laughing at himself. He had been reading Byron, and it reminded him of the way the poet sometimes wound up a stanza with a cynic phrase; and he could not enjoy this in bird or poet. Those birds were children of the sun, he said to himself. Before, if not above, all birds and all creatures, he loved the sun. The only time when he mentioned again the little grey chapel that stood highest among the mountains was to conjecture that it was built near the site of a temple for sun-worship. There were large upright stones in an adjoining field that were said to have formed part of a sun temple; and he liked to remember that. It was the God, not of the old stones, but of the chapel, that descended upon him in his last illness.

For weeks he lay sick and wild with dreams of the night and fears of the day. He raged and accused himself of unpardonable heresies, and defiance alternated with remorse. He was placid only when he whistled over and over again with unearthly sweetness and clearness, a fragment of one of the mountain songs of the blackbird, heard far away in the wild lands. It was a fantastic whim, for Whatever overpowered him in that friendless death-chamber, amid snow and silence, to wrest such blasting discords of an instrument that had seemed in the lane to know only natural joy and tranquillity. 'The little God,' he said, in one of his latest moments of relief, 'the little God torments me.' And again: 'But I go to the Great One. It is well.'

Friend of the blackbird, is it well? ('The Friend of the Blackbird', *The Last Sheaf*, 1928, 205–14)

The Chiffchaff – 'March the Third' (March 1915, *Last Poems*)

> Here again (she said) is March the third
> And twelve hours singing for the bird
> 'Twixt dawn and dusk, from half past six
> To half past six, never unheard.
>
> 'Tis Sunday, and the church-bells end
> When the birds do. I think they blend

Now better than they will when passed
Is this unnamed, unmarked godsend.

Or do all mark, and none dares say,
How it may shift and long delay,
Somewhere before the first of Spring,
But never fails, this singing day?

And when it falls on Sunday, bells
Are a wild natural voice that dwells
On hillsides; but the birds' songs have
The holiness gone from the bells.

This day unpromised is more dear
Than all the named days of the year
When seasonable sweets come in,
Because we know how lucky we are.

The Death of Winter

An oak had been felled on the coomb side, and a man
was clearing the brushwood round it, but the small bird's
double note, almost as regular as the ticking of a clock,
though often coming to an end on the first half, sounded
very clear in the coomb. He sang as he flitted among the
swaying ash tops in that warm, cloudy sun. I thought he
sang more shrilly than usual, something distractedly. But I
was satisfied. Nothing so convinces me, year after year, that
Spring has come and cannot be repulsed, though checked
it may be, as this least of songs. In the blasting or drip-
ping weather which may ensue, the chiffchaff is probably
unheard; but he is not silenced. I heard him on March 19
when I was fifteen, and I believe not a year has passed
without my hearing him within a day or two of that date. I
always expect him and always hear him. Not all the black-

birds, thrushes, larks, chaffinches, and robins can hide the note. The silence of July and August does not daunt him. I hear him yearly in September, and well into October the sole Summer voice remaining save in memory. But for the wind I should have heard him yesterday. I went on more cheerfully, as if each note had been the hammering of a tiny nail into Winter's coffin. (*In Pursuit of Spring*, extract from 'Guildford to Dunbridge', 91)

Song Birds – 'Something Fluttering in a Paper Bag'

The rain returned as I was crossing the railway bridge by Haydon's Road station. It was raining hard when the gypsy left the 'Sultan,' and still harder when I turned to the right along Merton Road. Rather than be soaked thus early, I took the shelter offered by a bird-shop on the left hand. This was not a cheerful or a pretty place. Overhead hung a row of cages containing chaffinches – battered ones at a shilling, a neater one at eighteen-pence – that sang every now and then, –

'My life and soul, as if he were a Greek.'

Inside the shop, linnets at half a crown were rushing ceaselessly against the bars of six-inch cages, their bosoms ruffled and bloody as if from the strife, themselves like wild hearts beating in breasts too narrow. 'House-moulted' goldfinches (price 5s. 6d.) were making sounds which I should have recognized as the twittering of goldfinches had I heard them among thistles on the Down tops. Little, bright foreign birds, that would have been hardly more at home there than here, looked more contented. A goldfish, six inches long, squirmed about a globe with a diameter of six inches, in the most complete exile imaginable. The birds at least breathed air not parted entirely from the south-west wind which was now soaking the street; but the fish was in a living grave. The place was perhaps more cheerless to look at than to live in, but in a short time three more persons took shelter by it, and after glancing at the birds, stood looking out at the rain, at the dull street, the tobacconist's, news-agent's, and confectioner's shops alone being unshuttered. Presently one of the three shelterers entered the bird-shop, which I had supposed shut; the proprietor came out for a chaffinch; and in a minute or two the customer left with an uncomfortable air and something fluttering in a paper bag such as would hold a penn'orth of sweets. He mounted a bicycle, and I after him, for the rain had forgotten to fall. He turned up to the left towards Morden station, which was my way also. Not far up the road he was apparently unable to bear the fluttering in the paper bag any longer; he got down, and with an awkward air, as if he knew how many great men had done it before, released the flutterer. A dingy cock chaffinch flew off among the lilacs of a garden, saying 'Chink'. The deliverer was up and away again. (*In Pursuit of Spring*, 42–4)

'The Thrush' (November 1915, *Last Poems*)
> When Winter's ahead,
> What can you read in November
> That you read in April
> When Winter's dead?
>
> I hear the thrush, and I see
> Him alone at the end of the lane
> Near the bare poplar's tip,
> Singing continuously.

Is it more that you know
Than that, even as in April,
So in November,
Winter is gone that must go?

Or is all your lore
Not to call November November,
And April April,
And Winter Winter – no more?

But I know the months all,
And their sweet names, April,
May and June and October,
As you call and call

I must remember
What died into April
And consider what will be born
Of a fair November;

And April I love for what
It was born of, and November
For what it will die in,
What they are and what they are not,

While you love what is kind,
What you can sing in
And love and forget in
All that's ahead and behind.

'A Bird in the Hand'

On a fine May morning hundreds of years ago in
Hampshire, three little boys went out to see what they

could see. Their names were Tommy Bowles, Jimmy Smith, and Jack Squibb. Tommy had the sharpest eye; Jimmy could climb best; Jack was the most patient. On and on they went, collecting here and there a thrush's or a blackbird's egg from hawthorn trees, once a jackdaw's from a hollow beech, once a robin's from the trouser pocket of a scarecrow, until they came to Petersfield Heath. There Jack found a linnet's nest with four eggs, and a lark's nest with a cuckoo's egg in it. Tommy climbed an elm and sat in the top, looking for the sea, and the ships at Portsmouth. Jimmy, who had grown tired of birds'-nesting was creeping among the furze after a pair of wrens. It was as hard to catch them as to catch a needle (a needle with legs and wings) in a haystack. But Jimmy kept on until Jack ran to his help; and still the wrens escaped them. When they reached the last furze-bush Tommy gave up looking for the sea and joined the hunt. They surrounded the bush. Jimmy lay down and looked up. Tommy knelt with his head inside the bush. Jack stood leaning over the top.

Whilst the three boys were in this position, all silent except Jimmy who had fallen asleep and was snoring, Farmer Guy walked across the heath towards them. He was carrying a goose swinging in his left hand. Seeing Tommy and Jack, and hearing Jimmy, he turned a little out of his path to learn what they were up to. 'What is it, boys?' he asked. 'Sh,' said Jack. 'Two jenny-wrens in the bush,' said Tommy. 'Are they as big as this?' asked the farmer, holding up the goose. 'No,' said Jack, 'but they are ours.' At the sound of this talking Jimmy awoke and rose up, and Tommy pulled his head out to see who was there. So they all stood round the bush waiting, and the wrens sat inside the bush waiting, and when the bells of Saint Peter's church struck nine, and a cuckoo in an elm said 'cuckoo' nine times, and Farmer Guy said: 'It's nine o'clock, boys, and I think a bird in the hand is worth two in the bush. Good-morning, and good luck to you, boys.' Then he went off on the foot-path to Goose Green. 'I believe they are still there,' whispered Jack to Tommy and Jimmy: but Tommy said: 'Didn't you hear what the old man said?' 'Yes,' said Jimmy, 'and I know where there's a hundred sand-martins' nests at Sheet.' 'Come on,' said Tommy. And they all set off. On the way Jimmy picked up a dead crow and carried it with him because he wanted the quills. Before they had got to Sheet they stopped to look at a poet from Sussex, who sat by a bramble-bush listening to two nightingales. The birds were close together inside the bush and took no more notice of the poet than he did of Tommy, Jimmy, and Jack. But the boys stared at the poet as hard as he stared at the birds. Jimmy was soon tired of this. 'Hi', said he to the poet, lifting up the dead crow, 'A bird in the hand is worth two in the bush'. Jack and Tommy laughed, and then Jimmy laughed; but as the poet took no notice of them they left him and went towards Sheet. On reaching the sand-martins' nests Jimmy threw away the crow.

As for the poet, when the nightingales began to fight instead of singing, he lay back in the grass and said to himself: 'For those that like dead crows and not living nightingales, a bird in the hand is worth two in the bush.' Many years afterwards in Oxfordshire he rode late at night up to an inn called 'The Bird in Hand,' kept by one John Squibb. Next morning he saw that the sign-board of the inn had a picture of a man carrying a crow, and he laughed, remembering the boys at Sheet. ('A Bird in the Hand is Worth Two in the Bush', *Four-and-Twenty Blackbirds,* 1915, 51–5)

Chapter Two

Flowers and Plants

As he loved individual birds and their changing song through the seasons and weather, Edward Thomas found pleasure in everyday plants and their emergence and appearance through the year. He recorded these seasonal patterns in his notebooks, and sometimes also in his prose; albeit in a more Romantic style. For instance, here he recorded the first signs of spring in 1913:

> By the side of the road were the first bluebells and cowslips. They were not growing there, but some child had gathered them below at Stowey or Durleigh, and then, getting tired of them, had dropped them. They were beginning to wilt, but they lay upon the grave of Winter. I was quite sure of that. Winter may rise up through mould alive with violets and primroses and daffodils, but when cowslips and blue-bells have grown over his grave he cannot rise again: he is dead and rotten, and from his ashes the blossoms are springing. (*In Pursuit of Spring*, 1914, 300)

Once again, it was common things that attracted Thomas's eye, their local names and the ways that they inspired his imagination. While Thomas gave us precise descriptions of plants and their habitats, he did not give us scientific classifications or precise locations. Perhaps this is because, as he explained with regard to historical knowledge in *The South Country*, '[b]etter a thousand errors so long as they are human than a thousand truths lying like broken snail-shells round the anvil of a thrush' (148). Like Wordsworth in the 'Preface' to the *Lyrical Ballads*, here Thomas hinted that systematic knowledge does not necessarily produce – in fact it can prevent – sympathy or concern. That said, Thomas's attitude towards scientific study is more complex than this suggests: as he explains in the earlier 'Nature-study' section of *The South Country*, knowledge is important for flourishing and happiness:

Knowledge aids joy by discipline, by increasing the sphere of enjoyment, by showing us in animals, in plants, for example, what life is, how our own is related to theirs, showing us, in fact, our position, responsibilities and debts among the other inhabitants of the earth. (144)

While the blood-red common poppy, or *Papaver rhoeas,* became a symbol of the trenches of the First World War, they were a traditional feature of the countryside in Western Europe, growing in disturbed earth. Poppies had long been seen as a symbol of fertility and the cycle of life through their association with crop plants and their prolific nature. Since the Second World War they have declined as a regular sight on British farmland due to agricultural intensification and the large-scale use of herbicides. Before any of this had happened, Edward Thomas talked about the emotional impact they produced – the 'uplifting of the heart' at their beauty and his feeling of separation from something so apparently full of life. In 'Poppies', Thomas echoed the Romantic attachment to the picturesque, but there is something different about Thomas's love of 'the commonwealth of living things'. Thomas loved landscapes that suggested long periods of human settlement, which allowed other species to thrive, and the processes of decay, renewal, and succession that were also part of this. He enjoyed plants with human associations, and humans that were marked by their relationship to the natural environment. In other places he described how plants would outlive us.

Nature in Literature – 'A Passionate and Mournful Love'

In our own day Nature has been used by many of the best writers of fiction as a magical background. It is hardly necessary to mention names, but those of Messrs. Hardy, Meredith, Hudson, Cunninghame Graham and Conrad will at once suggest their diversity. And it is becoming every year more and more characteristic of our literature to study this background of 'inanimate nature' and the animals for its own sake. Cowper's hare is interesting only because Cowper was fond of it and kind to it, Burns' mouse chiefly because it moved his passion; but it would not be hard to point to passages in the work of living men where the animal emerges free from any human taint, grand, wild, with all its savage perfume about it, in the desert attitude, and with a spiritual quality not of the writer's but of its own. The typical modern writer does actually suggest in written words that violent shock of the beautiful but inhuman which we have when suddenly the tall hare leaps across our path, or the dog fox's bark on the Downs makes twenty centuries of civilization nothing.

This interpretative literature has an immense field before it. There is no fact in Nature which some day it will not evoke into shining, melodious perfumed, tangible life. It is trying hard to do so; perhaps it is a little troubled by the size of the field. It denies no fact, just as it rejects no intuition. The best of its exponents have a sound knowledge of the facts of Nature and an inexorable curiosity, coupled, as they have hardly been before, with a deep and sometimes passionate and mournful love of all that takes place in the open air and in the human mind under its influence. They have, too, a curious interest in character – the character of birds, for example, of snakes, of places. Their writing adds considerably to pure knowledge, and, by their sense of the poetry in life, appeals to every one with an intellectual and spiritual life, whether naturalist or not; and it gives an interesting view of the mind of our age and continues the revelation which Jefferies began in *The Story of My Heart*.

(Excerpt from 'Introduction', *British Country Life in Spring and Summer: The Book of the Open Air*, 1907, v–vii)

Extract from Edward Thomas's Nature Diary in Swindon, Wiltshire: 'April – May 1895'

April 29 – Moschatel blossoming with its green fivefold flower.

Red-robin flowering in crowded ranks along the steep hedge-banks and in dank hollows.[9]

April 30 – Beech out in leaf with the sycamore, which begins to shower its green-yellow bloom on to the thin sward under.

May 2 – Orange-tip butterflies first seen, threading the coppice with a flight like blown leaves.

Early field scorpion-grass, a miniature hairy forget-me-not, blossoming from crannies in an old ha-ha: pale blue, earliest of its kind.

Mare's-tails not only grow in marshy land and even quite submerged, but in the driest spots, such as seldom-used railway embankments where the riddled chalk will not hold water an hour: here it grows, among the metals, with coltsfoot and wild carrot and poppy.[10]

May 3 – Coltsfoot down floating everywhere: the linnet takes it for her nest in the furze.

Dead-nettle flowers: found in January, June, and November. Cuckoo, courting with drooped wings, bobbing head and tail, and twisting body, with a laughing guttural 'coo-coo-coo-ga!'

Hum of bees loud round the stacked withy wands, golden with catkins that live long after the cutting of the branches.[11]

'I be fond of a crazy!' – the 'crazy' is the Wiltshireman's buttercup; so also, the marsh- marigold is the 'water-crazy'.

May 4 – Hedge-sparrows laying still.

Lesser whitethroat cradling his lightly woven nest in the blackthorn, whose blossom, mingling with the hawthorn boughs, is often taken for the may.

Sedge-warbler bathes singing in the rillets after rain.

May 6 – Oak-buds losing their nut-brown for the green of bursting leaves.

Buds more backward on the pollarded ash-trees than on the free-grown giants.

The linnets are breeding, but come in bands to the dandelions, whose flowerless husks they tear and empty.

Ribwort plantain blossoming.

Flycatchers arriving.

May 7 – Swifts unaccountably late, the weather having been mild throughout last month: at last they are here, screaming about their old turrets and familiar eaves.

May 8 – Waters strewn, as with scant driven snow, by waterweed blossoms.

Reed-bunting has a short peevish song, occasionally sweet; uttered from the top-most sprays of the hedge thorns.

Outer leaves of hawthorn partially bronze or deep red.

May 10 – Sedge-warblers laying: in rushes not often: usually in underwood near water: a nest built up inordinately high, but with no very deep hollow for the eggs.

Peonies in the cottage gardens.

Whinchat laying: five blue eggs, paler than the hedge-sparrow's, and having very few faint red stains. Nest, deeply hidden under the jags of an old willow at the root, built carelessly of grey bents, rootlets, moss, and little hair.

May 11 – Horse-chestnut thick with bloom: a week earlier in London.

Dragonflies abroad, spinning over the pools.

Reed-bunting has a nest of five eggs: built in the midst of rushes round which the outer bents are woven: coarsely needled, and large for the bird's size: framework of brittle grasses lined with black hair.

May 13 – Herb Robert flowering, with faint pink, rarely white; giving out an unpleasant odour from its dry downy leaves.

Laburnum founts of blossom.

Ash – leaves, bronzed before they are full-spread.

May 14 – Hawthorns covered up in bloom: a tardy blossoming, and the trees open their flowers one after another, some being thick with unopened buds in June.

Bird's-foot trefoil in gold-and-orange flower; a mere film of herbage on the parched chalk-downs, but several feet high in the damp hollows. The favourite lotus of Jefferies.

Oaks yellowed by slim catkins.

Comfrey or boneset blossoming with peals of white or purple bells over a mass of coarse foliage: kept in a hallowed corner of their gardens by the cottagers. ('In English Fields and Woods', *The Woodland Life*, 1897, 167–73)

Nettles and Ruins – 'Poppies'

The earliest mower had not risen yet; the only sign of human life was the light that burned all night in a cottage bedroom, here and there; and from garden to garden went the white owl with that indolent flight which seems ever about to cease, and he seemed to be the disembodied soul of a sleeper, vague, homeless, wandering, softly taking a dim joy in all the misty, dense forget-me-not, pansy, cornflower, Jacob's ladder, wallflower, love-in-a-mist and rose of the borders, before the day of work once more began.

So I followed the owl across the green and past the church until I came to the deserted farm. There the high-porched barn, the doorless stables, the cumbered stalls, the decaying house, received something of life from the owl, from the kind twilight or from my working mind. Above the little belfry on the housetop the flying fox of the weather vane was still, fixed for ever by old age in the south, recording not the hateful east, the crude and violent north, the rainy west wind. Whether because the buildings bore upon their surfaces the marks of many generations of life, all harmoniously continuous, or whether because though dead and useless they yet seemed to enjoy and could speak to a human spirit, I do not know, but I could fancy that, unaided, they were capable of inspiring afresh the idea of immortality to one who desired it. Mosses grew on the old tiles and were like moles for softness and rotundity. A wind that elsewhere made no sound talked meditatively among the timbers. The village Maypole, transported there a generation ago, stood now as a flagstaff in the yard, and had it burst into leaf and flower it would hardly have surprised. Billows of tall, thick nettle, against the walls and in every corner, were a luxuriant emblem of all the old careless ease of the labourers who, despite their sweat and anxiety and hopelessness, yet had time to lean upon their plough or scythe or hoe to watch the hounds or a carriage go by. Tall tansy and fleabane and hawkweeds and dandelions, yellow blossoms, stood for the bright joys of the old life. The campions on the hedge, the fumitory in the kitchen garden, meant the vague moods between sorrow and joy, speaking of them as clearly as when from out of the church flows the litany, charged with the emotion of those who hear it not though lying near. Had the wise owner admitted these things and for their sake obeyed the command of the will which bade him leave the Green Farm untouched? He might well have done so had he seen the birth of colour after colour in the dawn. At first, when doves began to coo and late cuckoos to call in invisible woods beyond, I thought that the green of grass was alive again; but that was only because I knew it was grass and could translate its grey. The green trees were still black above a lake of white mist far off when the yellows of hawkweed and tansy rose up. The purple fumitory, the blue of speedwells, came later. And then, as I turned a shadowy corner and came out into the broad half light just before sunrise, I saw the crimson of innumerable poppies that had a thought (sic) of mist pearl enmeshed amongst them.

They were not fifty yards away – they were in a well-known place – and yet there towered high walls and gloomed impassable moats between them and me, such was the strangeness of their beauty. Had they been reported to me from Italy or the East, had I read of them on a supreme poet's page, they could not have been more remote, more inaccessible, more desirable in their serenity. Something in me desired them, might even seem to have long ago possessed and lost them, but when thought followed vision as, alas! it did, I could not understand their importance, their distance from my mind, their desirableness, as of a far-away far-away princess to a troubadour. They were stranger than the high stars, as beautiful as any woman new-born out of summer air, though I could have reaped them all in half an hour. A book in a foreign, unknown language which is known to be full of excellent things is a simple possession and untantalising compared with these. They proposed impossible dreams of strength, health, wisdom, beauty, passion – could I but relate myself to them more closely than by wonder, as a child to a ship at sea which, after all, he may one day sail in, or of a lover for one whom he may some day attain. I was glad and yet I fatigued myself by a gladness so inhuman. Did men, I asked myself, once upon a time have simply an uplifting of the heart at a sight like this? Or were they destined in the end to come to that – a blissful end? Had I offended against the commonwealth of living things that I was not admitted as an equal to these flowers? Why could they not have vanished and left me with my first vision, instead of staying and repeating that it would be as easy to draw near to the stars as to them?

And yet the mind is glad, if it is troubled, of an impossible, far-away princess. She deceives the mind as Columbus deceived his weary sailors by giving out at the end of each day fewer knots than they had truly travelled, in order that they should not lose courage at the immensity of the voyage.

And still the poppies shone and the blackbird sang from his tower of ivory. (*The Heart of England*, 1906, 77–80)

Tall Nettles (May 1916, *Poems*)

> Tall nettles cover up, as they have done
> These many springs, the rusty harrow, the plough
> Long worn out, and the roller made of stone:
> Only the elm butt tops the nettles now.
>
> This corner of the farmyard I like most:
> As well as any bloom upon a flower
> I like the dust on the nettles, never lost
> Except to prove the sweetness of a shower.

'The Maiden's Wood'

At the upper end of a long beechen coombe that narrowed and wound and rose as it penetrated the hills, was a high ledge that looked southward down the coombe to a broad plain, an opposite range of bare and smooth hills, to other isolated hills seen above the lowest parts of the range, and, on a clear day, when the brain was tranquil and the eye at its full power, the sea beyond. This ledge was a few acres in extent, full of hollows and mounds and given up to beech, oak, and wild cherry, and it was protected from the north by a steep bank rising behind to the highest point on the hills. It was untouched by roads. The great highway that rose from the plain to the high land by a gradual ascent along the winding edge of the valley turned abruptly away from it. Once upon a time, indeed, a track had been worn from this high-way to a gravel pit under the steep bank; but the pit was overgrown with bushes and fern, and, as the way led nowhere beyond, it had long been disused. The land all round was poor and mostly wild. The few inhabitants went where they liked; and the footpaths were trodden so rarely that they were slender as hare-paths and hardly distinguishable from them, and none seemed to lead to the ledge, which I discovered by following the uneven track – where the branches did not turn me aside among the trees – in search of orchises. Once there I saw that it was traversed by many faint unreasonable paths leading into one another, which from a little distance could not be seen, for the foliage of dog's mercury, everywhere of equal height, gloomy and cool and tinged with a lemon hue, almost closed over the narrow grassless ribbons of brown earth and dead leaves, though once the feet rather than the eye had revealed them they were easily followed. If they had any centre of radiation it was an impenetrable thicket of brier and hazel all overlaced by the cordage of honey-suckle and traveller's joy, in the midst of which there were a few moss-covered rotten posts, all but one lying prone; and these, hardly different from the many dead and mossy stems of trees already decayed, did not arouse my curiosity.[12] One only of the paths was broad enough not to be mistakable. It ran along the brink of the ledge and appeared to have been artificially banked up. It was from here that the view was most perfect to the sea, or, on days less clear, to the long range and to the low plain, or merely to the wooded coombe where all the mists of the world seemed to be born and to return time after time like the sea. Once the ledge was left behind by only a few yards the view was gone, and nothing seen but the surface of the woods on the slopes below and the clouds on the blue over the topmost trees.

But the little wood was as a mountain kingdom apart, not merely on account of what could be seen from it and from it alone. It was divided from the woods of the coombe sides by earth walls, still high and once hedge-grown, like ancient fortifications; from the high lands behind by the precipitous bank; from the treeless trough of the coombe by the all but impassable steepness at the beginning of its descent. It was the home of the sun. East, south, and west, the sun never forgot it, and the twisted lean trees, many of them dead, did nothing to keep it out. So used was it to the sun just here, the great bee was careless of the heavy spring rain as he went feeling from white bloom to bloom of the dead-nettle.

The path at the brink was cut off short by the earth walls at either end. I thought that the whole ledge had been forgotten: the estates on these miles of half-precipitous wooded declivities were very large, and entirely neglected, the fallen trees lying where they fell because they were inaccessible; and there were no gamekeepers – what then could these two or three acres matter, even supposing that they were duly distinguished from the surrounding country on the maps locked up half a century ago by a lawyer? There were long days of every season when I believed it my own, or what was better even than posses-sion, I felt entirely free there and alone and without responsibility. I used to wander idly and without asking who the owner was, for I concluded that it had an owner in the sense that my occupation could be disputed if it were avowed. Day and night I used to go. In all those enormous woods there were only two sounds by day – the sudden laughs of the green woodpecker and the oceanic music of the wind which, even when it slept, seemed to dream there aloud. There was one other sound, but it was not often heard simply because it was always there, the noise of a streamlet running down among the woods; seldom did I notice it except in still cold nights when the huge forest hills were black and the sky starless and grey, and then the harsh sound was unceasing and ghostly, as of a river running in the sky. Once when the trees were all white under silent snow one heron came up the long empty coombe, grey and lean and slow and like a solitary ship entering the keel-less foam between the untrodden shores of some mighty estuary long ago; and he also was silent. But on that ledge between the forest and the high open land no bird was afraid to come, and whether that long kingdom of green leaves was roaring or silent I could always hear a bird singing among these trees or stirring the dead leaf. The stillest days of Spring, when the leaves could yet be numbered, were best savoured here where the enormous silence of the world was threaded by rivulets of song. By night there was the hoot and the shriek and the soft chuckling of the owls. Many a windy, cold night, dripping and black, I climbed up there and heard the owl crying his loudest and clearest into the echoing coombe, a strong happy voice when all other life but that in my own breast seemed to have passed away into the wind and rain.

Now and then I tried to picture the man or woman who had been there last. Whose were those footpaths? Or were these ribbons of earth, always bare among the green, not footpaths at all, but to be explained some other way?

I had been there a score of times without making anything like a full survey and inventory of my kingdom. It was becoming part of me, a kingdom rather of the spirit than of the earth, and I was content to see what I had seen on my first visit. In the neighbouring woods I had sought for orchises but after finding half a dozen kinds here at that time I had not looked for more. The other flowers were the usual flowers of the woods, the minute green moschatel, the stars of stitchwort and later woodruff, the bluebell and a few more, such as I was glad to greet for the twentieth time with more familiarity than ceremony. But one day I not only learnt that the wood was not my own, but that there was a further mystery. At the first moment the other visitor seemed to be its possessor, so much at home was she and so strange did I suddenly feel. It was a woman, how much past middle age I could not guess. Her hair was flaxen, her face as much weathered as it was possible to be without ceasing to be pink and fresh, her thin mouth at once childlike and shrewd, her eyes of a sparkling grey so that in each of them seemed always to be a drop of quicksilver sliding. She was short and plump and had a kind of briskness that I imagined to mean a nature of the utmost independence and unworldliness. She came towards me gathering flowers which she put into a basket on one arm. She looked at me with those intensely brilliant eyes that certainly saw me as I had never been seen before and saw in me something of which I was unaware; she curtsied and went on picking flowers. I was just about to step off the narrow path so as not to disturb her, when, still bending and without looking at me, she hopped aside and I passed by. Indeed I should not have spoken to this extraordinary human being, in spite of her rarity and fascination, if it had not been for the flowers which I caught sight of under her face. Though I am not a botanist I see most of the flowers in my path and I know the names of most; but I recognized none of these. They were bells and cups and stars clustered or single, in spires and bunches, that I had never seen growing wild before.

'There are many here in this wood,' she said in answer to my questions. 'Yes, only here.'

'Can you tell me their names?' I asked.

'No. They have never been christened that I know of,' she replied.

Seeing some orchises among them I said:

'But you know these?'

'Yes, they are fly-hawkins and butterflies' nests,' she said, perverting the names of the fly-orchis and bird's nest and butterfly orchises. She smiled, I did not know why; but it was a smile as fitting to her as her childlike mouth and complexion, her quick-silver eye, her briskness, and her hop to one side. I asked her the name of the wood. 'The Maiden's Wood,' – she said, 'It has always been called the Maiden's Wood. … I do not know the meaning of the name.' And she went on picking flowers. I now saw that these unfamiliar kinds were to be found everywhere in the little wood.

Twice again I saw her in the wood, and I liked to see her alone and undisturbed, at ease and at home there like a bird questing among the dead leaves when it has no fears of being observed.

Now that I saw the wood was not unknown I did not hesitate to ask questions at the nearest inn, several miles away, in the hope of learning more. I asked a young labourer. Yes, it had always been the Maiden's Wood. Old Mrs Malkin knew all about it, he said, for she went everywhere for flowers, and she got the curious ones in the Maiden's Wood, so they say – for he had never been there himself. I next asked an old man. He gave it the same name. There was a story, he said, but he did not belong to these parts, and he did not rightly remember it – something about a great lady, he believed, who had a garden there, hundreds of years ago it must have been. I asked him had there been a house there. No, no house; she did not live there; in fact he thought she was a ghost, though he had not seen it, or a fairy, or something.

Another old man said it was a queen had owned the place, he did not rightly know which queen, but she had stayed at the big manor house, now a farm, with the ancient wall round its orchard, which was the nearest building to the Maiden's Wood.

The farmer was a young man with a fine chestnut horse and a polished trap that was always rushing here and there on its bright yellow wheels. I hardly expected him to be able to tell me more. But I caught him out of his trap one day, having come to look at the wool in a barn where there was a boastful shearer who cut the flesh every minute in his effort to show himself the swiftest of his craft in the county, when he was being watched. The farmer was a practical man of few words, but he said that his father would be glad to have a talk, so he took me upstairs, backward and forward, as it seemed to me, the whole length and breadth and height of the big house that looked as if it had grown by some natural process of conglomeration, room by room; and at the top, in a corner no one could have suspected from the outside he showed me in to the old man. He was sitting in a high-backed chair, as stiff and as rugged as a tree, a huge grey-bearded man, as still as a tree too, for he could not rise to show his pleasure, which he did, however, by very soon setting out to talk very slowly in a voice that seemed to echo in his head before it left his lips, but without noticing any of my interruptions.

'I cannot tell you,' he said, 'when it was first called the Maiden's Wood, but I knew the Maiden. This was her room when she came to stay at the farm when I was a boy. The estate belonged to her and two brothers, this long bit from here up to the brow and that little bit you were speaking of as well, the Maiden's Wood. She was the Maiden. Some call it the Maiden's Garden. But her real garden was out there' – and looking out I saw a long wide border, under a fruit wall, full of flowers such as I had noticed in the wood – 'and it was her fancy to take the seeds out there into the wood and sow them there. She did it all herself. Many's the time, when they were ploughing up to the edge of the steep bank there, that they could see her down below in the wood as they were turning the horses round to begin another furrow. She used to walk up and down, up and down, and round and back again, rain or shine, no matter. She never had anyone with her there, and never would let anyone else go in except when we built the arbour for her in the middle of the wood: you have seen the posts of it, I dare say, but the thatch has gone long ago. Are the roses there now? I suppose not – oh, dear me, no, what am I thinking of? They would not last, pretty lady's roses they were with long Jerusalem names. She was pretty herself, too – not what everyone would like, you know, and some of them saw nothing in her, but like one of these ladies in pictures. She always wore the same kind of dress; like a maybush she looked in it, and one of the men seeing her and not knowing who it was took her for a blessed ghost. I was about eighteen then, and she was not any older. No. I liked to see her down there. But she wasn't our sort. Queer, something wrong or funny about her, and a well-born lady, too. The young have not any business to be like that. I never saw her speak to anyone. She always came here alone to stay. She used to talk to herself a lot, and it sounded as if she was saying poetry and lots of outlandish words out of books. She would have a book with her and hold it in her hand hanging down, as she walked back and forth. I laughed to myself about her many a time, I did. I and my brother helped to put up the arbour. It was her idea. What did a young thing want to be playing about by herself in the wood like that, I should like to know? It was the time of the Crimean war. She didn't care. I remember one day I was just turning the plough at the top by that bank above the Maiden's Wood when Jacob Stout went by galloping on the hard road a good mile away. He saw me and the team and he stopped his mare, and shouted 'Victory,' so that the horses pricked up their ears, wondering what was up, and off he went again. Now it so happened that Miss West was walking down below at the time, and having nobody to talk to after I had told the horses all about it and promised them an extra sieve of oats to eat Her Majesty's health with, I shouted 'Victory' myself, pretty loud. She stops dead, looks up at me, and says: 'John!' So I scrambles down, and there was she standing like a queen, and she gives me a crown. 'That's for the good news, John;' but I would sooner not have had it if only she had spared me the look she gave when she said, 'But I don't like to be disturbed, John.' I was feeling proud, too, and my view halloo used to be a good one, I promise you. You might have thought she was at her prayers, or courting. She might have been in love with somebody that had not the sense to love her back again – she was a beauty, dear me! such waste of time it was for her to be walking there all alone and looking for the sea, if you please. 'A clear morning, John,' she used to say some days, 'I ought to be able to see the sea this morning.' Funny thing. There was she with health and strength, riches and good looks, everything mortal wants, and not unhappy either, walking up and down among those trees just as if she was on a ship. She made those paths, every one of them, in her idleness. The only thing she ever *did* was to sow seeds there. She used to go out into the garden there after a warm day at harvest time and fill her pockets with seeds from her fancy plants, and then she would scatter them in the wood. It looked pretty for a time, but there are only a few left for

Jenny Malkin by this time, I doubt. It was not one year only – you might have understood that. These young ladies with nothing to do must have their whimsies. But one, two, three, four, five – the year I was married – yes! five years she was there, and all the spring and summer, half the autumn too, and Christmas time. What can you make of it? And then she did not come any more. The estate had to be sold. The brother went abroad. We missed her, too. She was kind and sensible in her talk; and then her looks did you good, ay! a bonny face. I never set eyes on her again. It was just after this we opened the gravel pit, and many a joke the men had about the arbour. The children found it out when they got a bit venturesome, and they pulled it about sadly. But after they began to work about the farm they never went more, not till my eldest went courting there, and then it was a rare sort of a lovers' nest for them all in a smother of weeds and climbers and roses, and the flowers there still; and when Mary came in wearing the pretty things I used to fall awondering what might have happened to Miss West that planted them. That must have been how it came to be called the Maiden's Wood, I should say. Albert and his sweetheart used to call it that, I recollect, and that is what we always call it.' ('The Maiden's Wood', *Rest and Unrest*, 1910, 145–63)

Seasonal Diary – 'Digging' (April 1915, *Last Poems*)

> Today I think
> Only with scents, – scents dead leaves yield,
> And bracken, and wild carrot's seed,
> And the square mustard field;

Odours that rise
When the spade wounds the root of tree,
Rose, currant, raspberry, or goutweed,
Rhubarb or celery;

The smoke's smell, too,
Flowing from where a bonfire burns
The dead, the waste, the dangerous,
And all to sweetness turns.

It is enough
To smell, to crumble the dark earth.
While the robin sings over again
Sad songs of Autumn mirth.

Spring

Nether Stowey begins with a church and a farm and farmyard in a group. Then follows a street of cottages without front gardens, dominated by a smooth green 'castle' rampart a third of a mile away. The street ends in a 'First and Last Inn' on one side, and a cottage on the other, announced as formerly Coleridge's by an inscription and a stone wreath of dull reddish brown. Altogether Nether Stowey offered no temptations to be compared with those of the road leading out of it. Immediately outside the village it was walled by deep banks, and on these grew arum, celandine, and nettle, with bushes of new-leaved blackthorn and spindle. Here I saw the first starry, white stitchworts or milkmaids. And henceforward I was always walking steeply up or steeply down one of the medley of lesser hills. Below on the right was chiefly red ploughland; above on the left wilder and wilder heights of sheep-fed moorland. The road was visible ahead, looping half way up the slopes.

Honeysuckle ramped on the banks of the deep-worn road in such profusion as I had never before seen. The sky had clouded softly, and the sun-warmed misty woods of the coombs, the noise of slender waters threading them, the exuberant young herbage, the pure flowers such as stitchwort and the pink and 'silver white' cuckoo flowers, but above all the abounding honeysuckle, produced an effect of wildness and richness, purity and softness, so vivid that the association of Nether Stowey was hardly needed to summon up Coleridge. The mere imagination of what these banks would be like when the honeysuckle was in flower was enough to suggest the poet. I became fantastic, and said to myself that the honeysuckle was worthy to provide the honeydew for nourishing his genius; even that its magic might have touched that genius to life – which is absurd. (*In Pursuit of Spring*, 1914, 271–73)

NOTES AND REFERENCES

9   Thomas probably meant 'ragged-robin' – *Lychnis flos cuculi*.
10 With regards to the 'mare's-tails': Thomas probably means what are commonly known as horsetails – *Equisetum* – although he is not the only person to confuse these two names. The term mare's-tail is generally used to refer to the unrelated genus *Hippuris*.
11 Withy wands are long, flexible branches of willow that are used for craft.
12 Traveller's joy is another name for old man's beard or *Clematis vitalba*.

Chapter Three

Footpaths and Roads

Thomas loved the ways that roads and paths connect us with earlier walkers, with other species, and with myths and pilgrimage; as Robert Macfarlane has noted, Thomas's roads are pathways for the imagination as well as for the feet.[13] His paths radiate outwards from his home in the south of England, to London, East Anglia, the West Country and Wales, via green lanes, footpaths, holloways, Roman Roads, metalled and unmade roads. He described the ancient route to St David's, the stretches of road in Wales known as Sarn Helen, the Pilgrims' Way to Canterbury, the Ridgeway and the Icknield Way. These routes connected him to the *Mabinogian*, to folklore and legends (see also Chapter Ten), to other writers, and to the labourers, soldiers, inn keepers, businessmen, gypsies and other wayfarers he met on route. He associated particular paths with friends he'd walked them with, and with the inns and pubs that allowed him a glimpse into other people's lives. On lonelier routes he found himself confronted with the ghosts of First World War casualties, and with his inner self, which he explored through various fictions of wanderers uncannily like himself (for more on these 'Others', see Chapter Six).

The extract from the 1909 work *The South Country* connects paths to Thomas's other interests – the traces of other human activities in the landscape: ploughing, sheep farming, burial. It also includes Thomas's plea to preserve the ancient paths from the activities of ruthless landowners and reckless tourism. Here, as elsewhere, Thomas emphasised the plight of gypsies, who had formerly camped on what were once-wide roadside verges, known as 'no-man's land'. These areas were, according to Thomas, being grubbed up by landowners, appropriated by the new rural district councils, or made unusable by the new roads. These new district councils replaced the earlier 'sanitary districts' and poor law districts, who dealt with public sanitation and poverty relief. Thomas was sympathetic to the gypsies, commoners and other wayfarers who depended on scraps of wild and common land for their livelihood.

❧❧❧❧❧

Roads – The Icknield Way

It is, however, in some ways a fitting book for me to write. For it is about a road which begins many miles before I could come on its traces and ends miles beyond where I had to stop. I could find no excuse for supposing it to go to Wales and following it there into the Ceidrych Valley, along the Towy to Caermarthen, and so to St. David's which is now as holy as Rome, though once only a third as holy. Apparently no special mediaeval use revived it throughout its course, or gave it a new entity like that of the Pilgrims' Way from Winchester to Canterbury that you and I walked on many a time – by the 'Cock' at Detling, the 'Black Horse' at Thurnham, the 'King's Head' (once, I believe, the 'Pilgrims' Rest') at Hollingbourne, above Harrietsham, past Deodara Villas, above Lenham and Robert Philpot's 'Woodman's Arms,' and so on to Eastwell; always among beech and yew and Canterbury bells, and always over the silver of whitebeam leaves.

I could not find a beginning or an end of the Icknield Way. It is thus a symbol of mortal things with their beginnings and ends always in immortal darkness. I wish the book had a little more of the mystery of the road about it. You at least will make allowances – and additions; and God send me many other readers like you. And as this is the bottom of the sheet, and ale is better than ink, though it is no substitute, I label this 'Dedication', and wish you with me inside the 'Dolau Cothi Arms' at Pumpsaint, in Caermarthenshire. (An excerpt from the dedication to *The Icknield Way*, 1913, vi–vii)

'Roads' (January 1916, *Last Poems*)

> I love roads:
> The goddesses that dwell
> Far along invisible
> Are my favourite gods.
>
> Roads go on
> While we forget, and are
> Forgotten like a star
> That shoots and is gone.
>
> On this earth 'tis sure
> We men have not made
> Anything that doth fade
> So soon, so long endure:
>
> The hill road wet with rain
> In the sun would not gleam
> Like a winding stream
> If we trod it not again.

They are lonely
While we sleep, lonelier
For lack of the traveller
Who is now a dream only.

From dawn's twilight
And all the clouds like sheep
On the mountains of sleep
They wind into the night.

The next turn may reveal
Heaven: upon the crest
The close pine clump, at rest
And black, may Hell conceal.

Often footsore, never
Yet of the road I weary,
 Though long and steep and dreary
As it winds on for ever.

Helen of the roads,
The mountain ways of Wales
And the Mabinogion tales,
Is one of the true gods,

Abiding in the trees,
The threes and fours so wise,
The larger companies,
That by the roadside be,

And beneath the rafter
Else uninhabited

Excepting by the dead;
And it is her laughter

At morn and night I hear
When the thrush cock sings
Bright irrelevant things,
And when the chanticleer

Calls back to their own night
Troops that make loneliness
With their light footsteps' press,
As Helen's own are light.

Now all roads lead to France
And heavy is the tread
Of the living; but the dead
Returning lightly dance:

Whatever the road bring
To me or take from me,
They keep me company
With their pattering,

Crowding the solitude
Of the loops over the downs,
Hushing the roar of towns
And their brief multitude.

The Origins of Roads

Much has been written of travel, far less of the road. Writers have treated the road as a passive means to an end, and honoured it most when it has been an obstacle; they leave the impression that a road is a connection between two points which only exists when the traveller is upon it. Though there is much travel in the Old Testament, 'the way' is used chiefly as a metaphor. 'Abram journeyed, going on still toward the south', says the historian, who would have used the same words had the patriarch employed wings. Yet to a nomadic people the road was as important as anything upon it. The earliest roads wandered like rivers through the land, having, like rivers, one necessity, to keep in motion. We still say that a road 'goes' to London, as we 'go' ourselves. We point out a white snake on a green hill-side, and tell a man: 'That is going to Chichester'. At our inn we think when recollecting the day: 'That road must have gone to Strata Florida'. We could not attribute more life to them if we had moving roads with platforms on the sidewalks. We may go or stay, but the road will go up over the mountains to Llandovery, and then up again over to Tregaron. It is a silent companion always ready for us, whether it is night or day, wet or fine, whether we are calm or desperate, well or sick. It is always going: it has never gone right away, and no man is too late. Only a humorist could doubt this, like the boy in a lane who was asked: 'Where does this lane go to, boy?' and answered: 'I have been living here these sixteen years and it has never moved to my knowledge'. Some roads creep, some continue merely; some advance with majesty, some mount a hill in curves like a soaring sea-gull.

Even as towns are built by rivers, instead of rivers being conducted past towns, so the first settlements grew up alongside roads which had formerly existed simply as the natural lines of travel for a travelling race. The oldest roads often touch the fewest of our modern towns, villages, and isolated houses. It has been conjectured that the first roads were originally the tracks of animals. The elephant's path or tunnel through the jungle is used as a road in India today, and in early days the wild herds must have been invaluable for making a way through forest, for showing the firmest portions of bogs and lowland marshes, and for suggesting fords. The herd would wind according to the conditions of the land and to inclinations of many inexplicable kinds, but the winding of the road would be no disadvantage to men who found their living by the wayside, men to whom time was not money. Roads which grew thus by nature and by necessity appear to be almost as lasting as rivers. They are found fit for the uses of countless different generations of men outside cities, because, apart from cities and their needs, life changes little. If they go out of use in a new or a changed civilization, they may still be frequented by men of the most primitive habit. All over England may be found old roads, called Gypsy Lane, Tinker's Lane, or Smuggler's Lane; east of Calne, in Wiltshire, is a Juggler's Lane; and as if the ugliness of the 'uggle' sound pleased the good virtuous country folk, they have got a Huggler's Hole a little west of Semley and south of Sedgehill in the same county: there are also Beggar's Lanes and roads leading past places called Mock Beggar, which is said to mean Much Beggar. These little-used roads are known to lovers, thieves, smugglers, and ghosts. Even if long neglected they are not easily obliterated. On the fairly even and dry ground of the high ridges where men and cattle could spread out wide as they journeyed, the earth itself is unchanged by centuries of traffic, save that the grass is made finer, shorter, paler, and more numerously starred with daisies. But on the slopes down to a plain or ford the road takes its immortality by violence, for it is divided into two or three or a score of narrow courses, trenched so deeply that they might often seem to be the work rather of some fierce natural force than of slow – travelling men, cattle, and pack-horses. The name Holloway, or Holway, is therefore a likely sign of an old road. So is Sandy Lane, a name in which lurks the half-fond contempt of country people for the road which a good 'hard road' has superseded, and now little used save in bird's-nesting or courting days. These old roads will endure as long as the Roman streets, though great is the difference between the unraised trackway, as dim as a wind-path on the sea, and the straight embanked Roman highway which made the proverb 'Plain as Dunstable Road,' or 'Good plain Dunstable' – for Watling Street goes broad and straight through that town. Scott has one of these ghostly old roads in *Guy Mannering*. It was over a heath that had Skiddaw and Saddleback for background, and he calls it a *blind road* – 'the track so slightly marked by the passengers' footsteps that it can but be traced by a slight shade of verdure from the darker heath around it, and, being only visible to the eye when at some distance, ceases to be distinguished while the foot is actually treading it.'

The making of such roads seems one of the most natural operations of man, one in which he least conflicts with nature and the animals. If he makes roads outright and rapidly, for a definite purpose, they may perish as rapidly, like the new roads of modern Japanese enterprise, and their ancient predecessors live on to smile at their ambition. These are the winding ways preferred by your connoisseur today. 'Give me,' says Hazlitt, 'the clear blue sky over my head and the green turf beneath my feet, a winding road before me, and a three-hours' march to dinner – and then to thinking!' These windings are created by the undulating of the land, and by obstacles like those of a river – curves such as those in the High Street of Oxford, which Wordsworth called 'the stream-like windings of that glorious street'.[14] (*The Icknield Way*, 1–5)

[second extract]

More often in books we move, as I have said, from place to place as in a dream. But it is a dream in the *Mabinogion* which gives one of the most majestic scenes of travel. I mean the dream of the Emperor Maxen. He dreamed that he was journeying along a river valley towards its source, and up over the highest mountain in the world until he saw mighty rivers descending to the sea, and one of them he followed to a great city at its mouth and a vast castle in the city. At the end of his journey the dreaming Emperor found a girl so beautiful that when he awoke he could think of naught else, while years went by, except her beauty. He sent out pioneers to discover the road of his dream, and at last they brought him to the castle and the same girl Helen sitting in the hall of it. She became his bride, and he gave her three castles – one at Arvon in North Wales, one at Caerleon, and one at Caermarthen in the South. Then, says the tale, 'Helen bethought her to make high-roads from one castle to another throughout the Island of Britain. And the roads were made. And for this cause are they called the roads of Helen Luyddawc, that she was sprung from a native of this island, and the men of the Island of Britain would not have made these great roads for any save her.' It is natural to connect with this Helen the great ancient roads leading north and south across Wales known as Sarn Helen or Elen. Nothing could be more noble as the name of a mountain road than Sarn Helen or Helen's Causeway.

It suggests to the ordinary fanciful and unhistoric mind the British Helena, mother of the Emperor Constantine, and that it suggested this long ago is clear from the old identification of Helen Luyddawc with the only child of King Cole of Colchester. The name has more recently been explained as Sarn y Lleng, the Road of the Legions. Sir John Rhys insists upon Elen instead of Helen, and believes her to be one of the pagan goddesses of the dusk.[15] 'There is,' he says, 'a certain poetic propriety in associating the primitive paths and roads of the country with this vagrant goddess of dawn and dusk.' These wandering paths are to the hard white highways what dusk is to the full blaze of day. First perhaps trodden by the wild herd and still without terrors for it, they might well be protected by a sort of Artemis, goddess of wildernesses and of forked ways, kind both to human hunters and the wild quarry. They belong to the twilight of the world. No doubt the sun shines no brighter at noon than it did then on a perfectly wild earth, on flowers that were never gathered, on bright plumage that no man had coveted. But all the forest and marsh of primeval earth form in the imagination mists to which the lack of history adds yet another veil. These mists lie over the world, to my mind, exactly as the white mist of summer lies, turning into a sea most of what once was land and making islands of the woods on the steep, uncultivated tracts. The islands rising out of the mists of time are the hills and mountains, and along their ridges ran the first roads, and by them are the squares and circles of the first habitations and the mounds of the first solemnized graves, used sometimes, it is thought, as guides for travellers.

It is particularly easy to think of Southern England as several chains of islands, representing the Downs, the Chilterns and Gog Magogs, the Mendips, Cotswolds and Quantocks. I have more than once caught myself thinking of the broad elephantine back of Butser Hill heaving up, spotted with gorse but treeless, between Petersfield and Portsmouth, as Ararat, though my unfaithful eyes fail to imagine the ark. There are days now when the clear suddenly swelling hills like Tarberry or Barrow Hill in Hampshire, or Cley Hill or the Knolls of Maiden Bradley in Wiltshire, or the abrupt promontories like Chanctonbury or Noar Hill near Selborne, or the long trooping ranges, seem to be islands or atolls looming dimly through the snowy still mists of morning or the clouds of rainstorm. Even without mist some of the isolated green hills rise out of the pale levels of cornland as out of sea; and I have seen, from near Bruton, the far-distant mass of Cadbury, the hill some call Camelot in Somerset, look like a dark precipitous isle. (*The Icknield Way*, extract from Chapter One, 'On Roads and Footpaths', 7–9)

'Women he liked' (June 1916, *Poems*)

> Women he liked, did shovel-bearded Bob,
> Old Farmer Hayward of the Heath, but he
> Loved horses. He himself was like a cob,
> And leather-coloured. Also he loved a tree.
>
> For the life in them he loved most living things,
> But a tree chiefly. All along the lane
> He planted elms where now the stormcock sings That
> travellers hear from the slow-climbing train.
>
> Till then the track had never had a name
> For all its thicket and the nightingales
> That should have earned it. No one was to blame.
> To name a thing beloved man sometimes fails.

Many years since, Bob Hayward died, and now
None passes there because the mist and the rain
Out of the elms have turned the lane to slough
And gloom, the name alone survives, Bob's Lane.

Footpaths – On Vanishing Paths

In the middle of the wood is a four-went way, and the grassy or white roads lead where you please among tall beeches or broad, crisp-leaved shining thorns and brief open spaces given over to the mounds of ant and mole, to gravel pits and heather. Is this the Pilgrims' Way, in the valley now, a frail path chiefly through oak and hazel, sometimes over whin and whinberry[16] and heather and sand, but looking up at the yews and beeches of the chalk hills? It passes a village pierced by straight clear waters – a woodland church – woods of the willow wren[17] – and then, upon a promontory, alone, within the greenest mead wrippled up to its walls by but few graves, another church, dark, squat, small-windowed, old, and from its position above the world having the characters of church and beacon and fortress, calling for all men's reverence. Up here in the rain it utters the pathos of the old roads behind, wiped out as if writ in water, or worn deep and then deserted and surviving only as tunnels under the hazels. I wish they could always be as accessible as churches are, and not handed over to land-owners – like Sandsbury Lane near Petersfield – because straight new roads have taken their places for the purposes of tradesmen and carriage people, or boarded up like that discarded fragment, deep-sunken and overgrown, below Colman's Hatch in Surrey. For centuries these roads seemed to hundreds so necessary, and men set out upon them at dawn with hope and followed after joy and were fain of their white-

ness at evening: few turned this way or that out of them except
into others as well worn (those who have turned aside for
wantonness have left no trace at all), and most have been well
content to see the same things as those who went before and
as they themselves have seen a hundred times. And now they,
as the sound of their feet and the echoes, are dead, and the
roads are but pleasant folds in the grassy chalk. Stay, traveller,
says the dark tower on the hill, and tread softly because your
way is over men's dreams; but not too long; and now descend
to the west as fast as feet can carry you, and follow your own
dream, and that also shall in course of time lie under men's
feet; for there is no going so sweet as upon the old dreams of
men. (*The South Country*, 1909, 59–60)

'The Path' (March 1915, *Poems*)

> Running along a bank, a parapet
> That saves from the precipitous wood below
> The level road, there is a path. It serves
> Children for looking down the long smooth steep,
> Between the legs of beech and yew, to where
> A fallen tree checks the sight: while men and women
> Content themselves with the road and what they see
> Over the bank, and what the children tell.
> The path, winding like silver, trickles on,
> Bordered and even invaded by thinnest moss
> That tries to cover roots and crumbling chalk
> With gold, olive, and emerald, but in vain.
> The children wear it. They have flattened the bank
> On top, and silvered it between the moss
> With the current of their feet, year after year.
> But the road is houseless, and leads not to school.
> To see a child is rare there, and the eye
> Has but the road, the wood that overhangs
> And underyawns it, and the path that looks

As if it led on to some legendary
Or fancied place where men have wished to go
And stay; till, sudden, it ends where the wood ends.

On Rights of Way

The road mounts the low Downs again. The boundless stubble is streaked by long bands of purple-brown, the work of seven ploughs to which the teams and their carters, riding or walking, are now slowly descending by different ways over the slopes and jingling in the rain. Above is a Druid moor bounded by beech-clumps, and crossed by old sunken ways and broad grassy tracks. It is a land of moles and sheep. At the end of a shattered line of firs a shepherd leans, bunched under his cape of sacking, to watch his black-faced flock dull-tinkling in the short furze and among the tumuli under the constant white rain. Those old roads, being over hilly and open land, are as they were before the making of modern roads, and little changed from what they were before the Roman. But it is a pity to see some of the old roads that have been left to the sole protection of the little gods. One man is stronger than they, as may be known by any one who has seen the bones, crockery, tin and paper thrown by Shere and Cocking into the old roads near by as into a dust-bin; or seen the gashes in the young trees planted down Gorst Road, Wandsworth Common; or the saucy 'Private' at the entrance to a lane worn by a hundred generations through the sand a little north of Petersfield; or the barbed wire fastened into the living trees alongside the footpath over a neighbouring hill that has lately been sold. What is the value of every one's right to use a footpath if a single anti-social exclusive landowning citizen has the right to make it intolerable except to such as consider it a place only for the soles of the feet? The builder of a house acquires the right to admit the sunlight through his window. Cannot the users of a footpath acquire a right, during the course of half-a-dozen dynasties or less, to the sight of the trees and the sky which that footpath gives them in its own separate way? At least I hope that footpaths will soon cease to be defined as a line – length without breadth – connecting one point with another. In days when they are used as much for the sake of the scenes historic or beautiful through which they pass as of the villages or houses on this hand or that, something more than the mere right to tread upon a certain ribbon of grass or mud will have to be preserved if the preservation is to be of much use, and the right of way must become the right of view and of very ancient lights as well. By enforcing these rights some of the mountains of the land might even yet be saved, as Mr. Henry S. Salt wishes to save them.[18] In the meantime it is to be hoped that his criticisms will not be ignored by the tourists who leave the Needle Gully a cascade of luncheon wrappings and the like; for it is not from a body of men capable of such manners that a really effective appeal against the sacrifice of 'our mountains' to commercial and other selfishness is like to spring.

And those lone wayside greens, no man's gardens, measuring a few feet wide but many miles in length – why should they be used either as receptacles for the dust of motor-cars or as additions to the property of the landowner who happens to be renewing his fence? They used to be as beautiful and cool and fresh as rivers, these green sisters of the white roads – illuminated borders of many a weary tale. But now, lest there should be no room for the dust, they are turning away from them the gypsies who used to camp there for a night. The indolent District Council that is anxious to get rid of its difficulties – for the moment – at the expense of a neighbouring district – it cares not – will send out its policemen to drive away the weary horses and sleeping children from the acre of common land which had hitherto been sacred – to what? – to an altar, a statue, a fountain, a seat? – No! to a stately notice-board; half-a-century ago the common of which this is a useless patch passed on easy terms to the pheasant lords. The gypsies have to go. Give them a pitch for the night and you are regarded as an enemy of the community or perhaps even as a Socialist. (*The South Country*, 255–57)

The Ridgeway – Oxfordshire, Berkshire and Wiltshire

The Blowingstone is a block of brown, iron-like sarsen stone standing on end, and of such a height that a man can bend over and comfortably blow into the mouth-piece at the upper side. This natural mouthpiece is the small roundish entrance to a funnel through the stone which emerges at a larger hole lower down at the back. A well-breathed person blowing bugle-fashion can make a booming that is said even now to carry five miles, if sustained for some time. At the hilltop, where it stood before it became a procurer of charity, a skilled and deep-chested hillman might have made himself heard much farther. From this hilltop, nearly seven hundred feet high, the Ridgeway rises to its greatest height. Hitherto it had hardly ever had higher land on either side of it for very many miles. At Uffington Castle it is over eight hundred feet high, but a little lower than the highest part of the camp.[19] From the rampart about this circle of almost level turf I could see the Quarley Hill range and far over the Lambourn Downs to Martinsell Hill by Savernake; I could see Barbury Castle and the wooded hills of Clyffe and Wroughton, and Badbury, the Cotswolds, the Oxfordshire hills, Sinodun, and the Chilterns. The Dragon

Hill below it is an isolated eminence shaped like the butt of an oak tree, and similar to that one in the hollow between Gramp's and Hackpen hills, but ruder and more distinct.

Past the south and lower side of Uffington Castle the Ridgeway went fairly straight, with a thorn or two on either side, towards the thick beech clump above Wayland's Smithy, sometimes a green road, sometimes worn white. The hill-side was divided among charlock and different greens in squares and triangles, and here and there a thatched barn or rick at a comer. Southward I saw the pleasant, dappled scatter of Knighton Bushes[20] over the turf, sometimes considerable woods like those of Ashdown by Alfred's Castle; in several places the long stretch of turf reared itself up with beautiful but detached hills, like Tower Hill, as high as the main ridge. The hot, misty sun drew out all the odour from uncut grass, clover, cocks-combs, yellow bedstraw, ox-eye daisies, and bird's-foot trefoil, and the light air mixed them. Whatever was visible or hid on the left, the road always commanded the northward valley, the main expanse, and also for the most part the nearer land where the villages lay, close to the foot of the hills on which it was travelling. An enemy might have lain or moved concealed within a very short distance on the south, but never on the north, and it might be conjectured, therefore, that attack was to be feared from that side only, and that the other was friendly country to those most commonly upon the road. The camps of Lowbury, Letcombe, and Uffington were all to northward; Alfred's Castle alone was on the south, at Ashdown, among the greatest woods now surviving on this part of the Downs. It is hardly possible for unhistorically minded men to think of war on these hills, unless troops are manoeuvring over them. Yet the Ridgeway is like nothing so much as a battlement walk of superhuman majesty. The hills between Streatley and

Liddington form a curve in the shape of a bow, a doubly curved Cupid's bow. Following this line, always keeping at the edge of the steep north-ward slope and surveying the valley, the Ridgeway carries the traveller for thirty miles as if along the battlements of a castle. He begins at Streatley by having the early morning sun of spring over his right shoulder; the full light of midday is on his left as he passes Letcombe Castle; the sun is going down on his right hand as he descends to Totterdown and the pass for the Roman road and modern traffic between the hills.

It is still debated whether most or little of the down-land was once covered with trees. Those recently planted on very high places have often failed to make more than a spindly and ruinous growth, as at Chanctonbury Ring, Liddington Hill, and Barbury. But wherever there is a tertiary deposit beech and oak, not to speak of lesser trees, abound and even flourish in great size and noble forms. Gorse, hawthorn, and elder rapidly take posses-sion anywhere of neglected ground, and make an impene-trable scrub. Yews expand and beeches grow tall and close on steep and almost precipitous slopes where the chalk is easily bared by rain, traffic, or rabbits. There is thus some reason for thinking that the open downland is largely the product of cultivation and nibbling flocks.

The flocks no longer feed much on the hills, and, except when folded in squares of turnips or mustard, are seldom seen there. They have become more and more a kind of living machinery for turning vegetables into mutton, and only in their lambhood or motherhood are they obviously of a different tribe from sausage-machines, etc. In time, with the discovery of a way of concentrating food and sunlight and of adapting the organs of the sheep to these essences, it will be possible to dine carnivorously on

Sunday upon what was grass on Friday; but 'for ever climbing up the climbing wave', men shall sigh for lambs born filleted with a double portion of sweetbreads.[21]

From Uffington Castle the road descended slowly, and reached six hundred feet at the Wiltshire border, a third of a mile past the road from Idstone to Ashdown. Then gradually it rose towards a point much above seven hundred feet between two distinct breasts of down south-westward. In places it had a good hedge of thorn, maple, and brier on one side, at others only isolated little thickets of thorn, brier, and black bryony, or groups where the last May-blossom met the first guelder roses. Once at a corner before Ridgeway Farm five beeches stood together making a shadow. The highest point showed me the beeches of Liddington clump, each stem distinct, the fall of clear turf down to the plain, and beyond that the Barbury clump and the long down wall bending to Avebury. (*The Icknield Way*, 263–67)

Immortality

The footpath by the mill was fading away, for it now led to nowhere – whither few cared to follow it. Possibly the last step may soon linger among the encroaching flowers, the rank growths of willow-herb, tansy, and betony which, poor enough by themselves, make the thicket sumptuous by their profusion. And who took the first step? Someone in the days when, wherever you went you came to nowhere. For there are few footpaths that are new, and those that are old may be drowned or cut to pieces, or may be incorporated (as De Quincey has said) in someone's kitchen, but seem never to die, and the more they are down-trodden the more they flourish. Curiosity as to whether Shakespeare ever started one is idle. They are footprints, perhaps, of the immortals. They are vestiges of that older day when this land also 'was in Arcady'. Even today they may be seen, after rising and falling in the fields, to be gathered into that far country again, where hills like clouds and clouds like hills are mingled beneath the white sun of noon. (Extract from 'Isoud with the White Hands', *Horae Solitariae*, 179–180)

City walks – Leaving London

Then I set out and began to stain the immense silence of the city with the noise of my heels and stick. A journalist or two went by; a fat man and his fat dog straying from the neat bar of a Conservative Club homewards without precipitancy; a few pleasure-seekers with bleared or meditative eye; a youth with music in his steps, fresh from some long evening of talk and song, perhaps his first. Here was a policeman stern and expectant in a dark entry, or smoking a pipe; there stood or sat or leaned or lay men and women who no more give up their secrets than the blinded windows and the doors that will not be knocked at for hours yet. How noble the long, well-lighted streets at this hour, fit with their smooth paved ways for some roaring game, and melancholy because there is no one playing. The rise and fall of the land is only now apparent. In the day we learn of hills in London only by their fatigue; in the night we can see them as if the streets did not exist, as they must have appeared to men who climbed them with a hope of seeing their homes from the summits or of surprising a stag beneath. The river ran by, grim, dark and vast, and having been untouched by history, old as hills and stars, it seemed from a bridge, not like a wild beast in a pit, but like a s- trange, reminiscential amulet, worn by the city to remind her that she shall pass. How tameless and cold the water, alien, careless, monstrous, capable of drowning in a little while the uttermost agony or joy and making them as if they had never been. I passed by doors where lived people whom I knew, but it was two o'clock in the morning; they could not know me. I wondered which of them I could safely disturb. With what expression would they come down from their warm beds and oblivion, with dull, puzzled eyes, and slowly recall those things which – even the pleasant ones – our lonely lives so often reduce to mere entries in a tedious chronicle. I left the question unanswered.

Now I saw a tall, stiff crane surmounting the houses and nodding in the sky, itself simple, strong, direct, weighing the city against the heavens in an enormous balance with Rhadamanthine solemnity.

Endless were the vast caves and deserts of the streets, most strange the unobserved, innumerable things prepared for the eyes of men on the coming day – glittering windows of cutlery, food, drugs, sadlery – the high walls with coloured advertisements of beer, medicine, food, actors, newspapers, corsets, concerts, pickles. The dark windows, the windows lit to serve some purpose unknown, seemed to make it necessary to cry out, to raise an alarm, to make sure that the darkness or light meant only the usual things. Now and then several streets ran towards one another and left a square or irregular space at their meeting, surrounded by an inn with a sign, a stone trough, an old eighteenth-century house, its windows emphasised by white paint, a row of pollarded limes, a scrap of orchard – once perhaps the heart of a village. Or for almost a mile the streets ran straight, with branches at right angles, and suddenly a large house stood back and its garden of limes and lawn broke the monotone. The names of the streets were an epitome of the world and time, commemorating famous and unknown men, battles, conspiracies, far-off cities and rivers, little villages known to me, streams and hills now buried by houses; the names of the inns were as rich as the titles of books in an old library, suggested many an inn by wood and mill and meadow and village square, but all confused as if in a marine store. And as I walked through old and new villages, rents, courts, alleys, lanes, rises, streets, buildings, roads, avenues, I seemed to be travelling through the Inferno and Purgatorio, but before the first man had entered them and without a guide. It was immense, sublime, but its purposes dark and not to be explained by the policemen here and there in charge. Nor, passing through Battersea, did I meet the famous man who has threaded this mystery. He, at least, would have taken me to a housetop and have unravelled space; but I expected him at street corners and on commons in vain. But presently I reached a sign-post that stood boldly up with undoubted inscriptions, one of them to London, and away from that I set my face, though I saw market-carts going the way I had come, with drowsy carters, one lamp, and horses whose shadowy muscles quivered in the electric light. That sign-post seemed to make all things clear. Like a prophet it rose up, who after an age of darkness says that the path of life and goodness is plain, that he knows it, and that all who follow him will be saved. Not for him hesitation and qualification; but to all men perplexed by definitions, testimonies, other prophets and their own thoughts, he cries: 'This is the way'.

'The world may find the Spring by following her.'[22]

I followed and needed only a good marching song. By chance I lighted on one which was first sung by countrymen. It is not triumphant – the mind wearies of a triumphant song in solitude and at night – but it persists and acknowledges no end. It was made by feeble, mighty-limbed men who knew what it is to go on and on for ends which they do not entirely apprehend. It matches the hurrying feet of the lover or the limp of the hungry man at dawn. It begins: –

> With one man, with two men,
> We mow the hay together;
> With three men, with four men,
> We mow the hay together:
> With four, with three, with two, with one, no more.
> We mow the hay and rake the hay and take it away
> together.

It goes on: —

> With five men, with six men,
> We mow the hay together;
> With seven men, with eight men,
> We mow the hay together;
> With eight, with seven, with six, with five, with four,
> with three, with two, with one, no more,
> We mow the hay and rake the hay and take it away
> together.

It goes on until a hundred is reached, proceeding after twenty by tens. And so, gradually, as the song went on, the houses opened apart, and the road ahead was a simple white line. (*The Heart of England*, 7–11)

NOTES AND REFERENCES

13 Robert Macfarlane, *The Old Ways* (London, 2012).
14 William Wordsworth, 'Oxford', *Miscellaneous Sonnets* XXXI.
15 Thomas's footnote: 'Hibbert Lectures, 1889, p. 16'.
16 Gorse and bilberry.
17 'Willow wren' is another name for a willow warbler.
18 Thomas's note: 'see his valuable *On Cambrian and Cumbrian Hills* (Fifield)'.
19 Uffington 'castle' is an Iron Age hill fort.
20 Knighton Bushes is the site of an ancient settlement and field system.
21 Thomas quotes from Tennyson's 'The Lotos-eaters'
22 Thomas quotes from 'Aeglamour's Lament', by Ben Jonson.

Chapter Four

The Historic Landscape

When Edward Thomas became a writer his countryside writing was influenced by his earlier passion for natural history. In terms of his approach to history, Gilbert White's *The Natural History of Selborne* was perhaps the most important influence. The 18th century curate based his work on his own nature diaries and intimate knowledge of the parish of Selborne in Hampshire, and the final extract in this chapter, 'The Brook', returns us to Hampshire.

One of the features of the landscape features that interested Thomas – more than castles or cathedrals – were barrows, or tumuli, which are raised earth and stones set over a grave or graves. He believed that these simple and ancient landscape features – along with footpaths, roads, and ruins – offered imaginative symbols. While the tumuli are partly symbols of death, like the epitaphs on graves and monuments he often noted, they reanimate the past for the imagination through their physical presence in ways that facts or statistics can not.

Thomas's 'environmental history' approach in the essay 'Chalk Pits' from *The Last Sheaf* showed that there is no such thing as 'wilderness' when it comes to the English countryside. Discussing the chalk pits around the south of England, Thomas observed that the places that were marginal for agriculture or industry had long-been a sanctuary for wildlife and certain groups of people. Chalk had been used in agriculture as a soil improver for acid or sandy soil; and before then it had been used as a building material. Once chalk pits were abandoned due to modern agricultural methods, they became home to the succession of plant species that thrive in newly abandoned places. Our modern equivalents of these locations would be the wildernesses surrounding power stations or former military sites, which are increasingly being designated as wildlife reserves. Chalk pits – as well as other types of mines – provided Thomas with a surprisingly attractive and evocative subject matter.

History – History and the Parish

Some day there will be a history of England written from the point of view of one parish, or town, or great house. Not until there is such a history will all our accumulations of information be justified. It will begin with a geological picture, something large, clear, architectural, not a mass of insignificant names. It must be imaginative: it might, perhaps, lean sometimes upon Mr. Doughty's *Dawn in Britain*. The peculiar combination of soil and woodland and water determines the direction and position and importance of the ancient trackways; it will determine also the position and size of the human settlements. The early marks of these – the old flint and metal implements, the tombs, the signs of agriculture, the encampments, the dwellings – will have to be clearly described and interpreted. Folk-lore, legend, place-names must be learnedly, but bravely and humanly used, so that the historian who has not the extensive sympathy and imagination of a great novelist will have no chance of success. What endless opportunities will he have for really giving life to past times in such matters as the line made by the edge of an old wood with the cultivated land, the shapes of the fields, with their borders of streams or hedge or copse or pond or wall or road, the purpose and interweaving of the roads and footpaths that suggest the great permanent thoughts and the lesser thoughts and dreams of the brain ... As the historic centuries are reached, the action of great events, battles, laws, roads, invasions, upon the parish – and of the parish upon them – must be shown. Architecture, with many of its local characteristics still to be traced, will speak as a voice out of the stones of castle, church, manor, farm, barn and bridge. The birds and beasts cannot be left out. The names of the local families – gentle and simple – what histories are in them, in the curt parish registers, in tombstones, in the names of fields and houses and woods. (*The South Country*, 147–48)

Cornwall

All along the coast (and especially where it is lofty and houseless, and on the ledges of the crags the young grey gulls unable to fly bob their heads seaward and try to scream like their parents who wheel far and near with double yodelling cry), there are many rounded barrows looking out to sea. And there are some amidst the sandhills, bare and corrugated by the wind and heaved up like a feather-bed, their edges golden against the blue sky or mangily covered by drab marram grass that whistles wintrily; and near by the blue sea, slightly roughened as by a harrow, sleeps calm but foamy among cinder-coloured isles; donkeys graze on the brown turf, larks rise and fall and curlews go by; a cuckoo sings among the deserted mines. But the barrows are most noble on the high heather and grass. The lonely turf is full of lilac scabious flowers and crimson knapweed among the solid mounds of gorse. The brown-green-grey of the dry summer grass reveals myriads of the flowers of thyme, of stonecrop yellow and white, of pearly eyebright, of golden lady's fingers, and the white or grey clover with its purest and earthiest of all fragrances. Here and there steep tracks descend slantwise among the thrift-grown crags to the sea, or promise to descend but end abruptly in precipices. On the barrows themselves; which are either isolated or in a group of two or three, grow thistle and gorse. They command mile upon mile of cliff and sea. In their sight the great headlands run out to sea and sinking seem to rise again a few miles out in a sheer island, so that they resemble couchant beasts with backs under water but heads and haunches upreared. The cliffs are cleft many times by steep-sided coves, some with broad sand and shallow water among purple rocks, the outlet of a rivulet; others ending precipitously so that the stream suddenly plunges into the black sea among a huddle of sunless boulders. Near such a stream there will be a grey farm amid grey outbuildings – with a carved wooden eagle from the wreckage of the cove, or a mermaid, once a figure-head with fair long hair and round bosom, built into the wall of a barn. Or there is a briny hamlet grouped steeply on either side of the stream which gurgles among the pebbles down to the feet of the bearded fisherman and the ships a-gleam. Or perhaps there is no stream at all, and bramble and gorse come down dry and hot to the lips of the emerald and purple pools. Deep roads from the sea to the cliff-top have been worn by smuggler and fisherman and miner, climbing and descending. Inland shows a solitary pinnacled church tower, rosy in the warm evening – a thin line of trees, long bare stems and dark foliage matted – and farther still the ridges of misty granite, rough as the back of a perch.

Of all the rocky land, of the sapphire sea white with quiet foam, the barrows are masters. The breaking away of the rock has brought them nearer to the sea as it has annihilated some and cut off the cliff-ways in mid-career. They stand in the unenclosed waste and are removed from all human uses and from most wayfaring. Thus they share the sublimity of beacons and are about to show that tombs also have their deaths. Linnet and stonechat and pipit seem to attend upon them, with pretty voices and motions and a certain ghastliness, as of shadows, given to their cheerful and sudden flittings by the solemn neighbourhood. But most of their hold upon the spirit they owe to their powerful suggestion that here upon the high sea border was once lived a bold proud life, like that of Beowulf, whose words, when he was dying from the wounds of his last victory, were: 'Bid the warriors raise a funeral mound to flash with fire on a promontory above the sea, that it may stand high and be a memorial by which my people shall remember me, and seafarers driving their tall ships through the mist of the sea shall say: "Beowulf's Mound"'.

In Cornwall as in Wales, these monuments are the more impressive, because the earth, wasting with them and showing her bones, takes their part. There are days when the age of the Downs, strewn with tumuli and the remnants of camp and village, is incredible; or rather they seem in the course of long time to have grown smooth and soft and kind, and to be, like a rounded languid cloud, an expression of Earth's summer bliss of afternoon. But granite and slate and sandstone jut out, and in whatsoever weather speak rather of the cold, drear, hard, windy dawn. Nothing can soften the lines of Trendreen or Brown Willy or Carn Galver against the sky. The small stone-hedged ploughlands amidst brake[23] and gorse do but accentuate the wildness of the land from which they have been won. The deserted mines are frozen cries of despair as if they had perished in conflict with the waste; and in a few years their chimneys standing amidst rotted woodwork, the falling masonry, the engine rusty, huge and still (the abode of rabbits, and all over-grown with bedstraw, the stern thistle and wizard henbane) are in keeping with the miles of barren land, littered with rough silvered stones among heather and furze, whose many barrows are deep in fern and bramble and foxglove. The cotton grass raises its pure nodding white. The old roads dive among still more furze and bracken and bramble and foxglove, and on every side the land grows no such crop as that of grey stones. Even in the midst of occasional cornfield or weedless pasture a long grey upright stone speaks of the past. In many places men have set up these stones, roughly squaring some of them, in the form of a circle or in groups of circles and over them beats the buzzard in slow hesitating and swerving flight. In one place the work of Nature might be mistaken for that of man. On a natural hillock stands what appears to be the ruin of an irregularly heaped wall of grey rock, roughened by dark-grey lichen, built of enormous angular fragments like the masonry of a giant's child. Near at hand, bracken, pink stonecrop, heather and bright gold tormentil soften it; but at a distance it stands black against the summer sky, touched with the pathos of man's hand-iwork overthrown, yet certainly an accident of Nature. It commands Cape Cornwall and the harsh sea, and St. Just with its horned church tower. On every hand lie cromlech, camp, circle, hut and tumulus of the unwritten years. They are confused and mingled with the natural litter of a barren land. It is a silent Bedlam of history, a senseless cemetery or museum, amidst which we walk as animals must do when they see those valleys full of skeletons where their kind are said to go punctually to die. There are enough of the dead; they outnumber the living; and there those trite truths burst with life and drum upon the tympanum with ambiguous fatal voices. At the end of this many-barrowed moor, yet not in it, there is a solitary circle of grey stones, where the cry of the past is less vociferous, less bewildering, than on the moor itself, but more intense. Nineteen tall, grey stones stand round a taller, pointed one that is heavily bowed, amidst long grass and bracken and furze. A track passes close by, but does not enter the circle; the grass is unbent except by the weight of its bloom. It bears a name that connects it with the assembling and rivalry of the bards of Britain. Here, under the sky, they met, leaning upon the stones, tall, fair men of peace, but half-warriors, whose songs could change ploughshare into sword. Here they met, and the growth of the grass, the perfection of the stones (except that one stoops as with age), and the silence, suggest that since the last bard left it, in robe of blue or white or green the colours of sky and cloud and grass upon this fair day the circle has been unmolested, and the law obeyed which forbade any but a bard to enter it. Sky-blue was the colour of a chief bard's robe, emblematic of peace and heavenly calm, and of unchangeableness. White, the colour of the Druid's dress, was the emblem of light, and of its correlatives, purity of conduct, wisdom, and piety. Green was the colour of the youthful ovate's robe, for it was the emblem of growth. Their uniformity of colour signified perfect truth. And the inscription upon the chair of the bards of Beisgawen was, 'Nothing is that is not for ever and ever'. Blue and white and green, peace and light and growth' – 'Nothing is that is not for ever and ever' – these things and the blue sky, the white, cloudy hall of the sun, and the green bough and grass, hallowed the ancient stones, and clearer than any vision of tall bards in the morning of the world was the tranquil delight of being thus 'teased out of time' in the presence of this ancientness. (*The South Country*, 156–61)

Chalk Pits – Southern England

It is sometimes consoling to remember how much of the pleasantness of the English country is due to men, by chance or design. The sowing of various crops, the planting of hedges and building of walls, the trimming of woods to allow trees to grow large and shapely, and so on, are among the designed causes of this pleasantness. Here men have obviously co-operated with Nature. But as great effects are produced when they have seemed at first to insult or ignore her. A new house, for example, however well proportioned, and however wisely chosen the material, is always harsh to the eye and mind. In a hundred years it little matters what the form or the material; if the house survives, and is inhabited for a century, it has probably made its place. If it is deserted, it makes a place yet more rapidly. There is no building which the country cannot digest and assimilate if left to itself about twenty years. Cottage or factory or mansion is powerless against frost, wind, rain, grass and ivy, and the entirely assimilated building is always attractive unless the beholder happens to know the reason why it was deserted; and even if he does, his sympathy will very likely not conflict with his sense of beauty, but will aid it in secret – that is what is consoling. London deserted would become a much pleasanter place than Richard Jefferies pictured it in *After London*. The mere thought of the jackdaws who would dwell there is a cheerful one, and they would not be alone. I like to think what mysteries the shafts, the tubes, the tunnels and the vaults would make, and what a place to explore. The railway cuttings, unless very steep-sided, soon become romantic, and near London they are a refuge for many plants and insects.

But among the works of men that rapidly become works of Nature, and can be admired without misanthropy, are the chalk and marl pits. The great ones are pleasing many miles away, both in themselves and through association. On a hillside they always assume a good shape, like those of a scallop shell or even of a fan. Those on the Downs above Lewes, Maidstone and Midhurst, will be remembered. Against their white walls we can like the limeworks themselves, whether they offer only the ordinary black chimneys as at Buriton, or whether they are majestic in their arched masonry like those which are consuming the Dinas above Llandebie in Carmarthenshire. If there were only one of these fans or scallops of white low down on a bare hillside it would be as celebrated as the inverted fan of Fujiyama in Japan. They are impressive, I think, chiefly as being, with the exception of glass-houses and sheets of water, the only distinctly luminous objects on the comparatively dark earth. They show up like arched windows or doorways of gigantic proportions lighted from within the hills. Their all but perpendicular walls take long to be grassed over when deserted, even if the rabbits do not seek refuge in them and keep the chalk moving by their narrow terraces. Perhaps that enormous scoop is one that has been so grassed over, on the steep hillside facing southward near East Meon. It is completely covered with fine grass, and has an almost level green floor, which is used as a playing field. It bears the name of 'The Vineyard,' and it has been suggested that it was used by the Romans or Romantized Britons for the cultivation of vines. But this is very much like one of the lesser natural coombes of the chalk country, and except for its name, and possible use, it has no particular interest. The lesser chalk pits are the better. They may be divided roughly into two kinds – first, those which are dug out of more or less level ground, and are shaped like a bowl or funnel, or a series of such; second, those which have been carved out of a slope. Those upon a slope are usually the more charming to the eye. They are met, for example, suddenly where the road bends round a steep bank, and whether the chalk is dazzling or shadowed it is welcome. The white or grey-white wall is over-hung by roots of ash and beech trees, and if it be old by a curtain of traveller's joy [see previous note] or ivy. These over-hanging roots and climbers often form a covered way large enough for a man to creep through, and much used by foxes and lesser beasts. At the foot is a waste space of turf. Here grows the wayfaring tree with its pendant clusters of cherry-coloured fruit, or the beam tree, whose leaves fall with their heavy sides uppermost and so lie all through the winter; or perhaps bracken and purple-stemmed angelica, nine feet high and straight, with graceful bracketed frondage all still; or perhaps the sweetest flowers of the chalk, the yellow St. John's wort, birdsfoot, agrimony, and hawkweed, the pink bramble and mallow, the mauve marjoram and basil, the purple knapweed, and to these come the Red Admiral and Peacock and Copper butterflies, the bright-winged flies and bees, and the grass-hoppers like emerald armoured horsemen – four white butterflies float past hundreds of flowers without heeding them, and then all four try to alight on one. The air is full of the sweetness of wild carrot and parsnip seeds. Sometimes the floor is filled up with a dense Paradise of bramble and blackthorn, and there is a nightingale in it or a blackcap and in the winter a wren.

The hollow pits are not so familiar, because they lie often in the middle of fields which they used to supply with chalk. They may be so shallow that they have been ploughed over, and now merely serve to break the surface of a great cornfield. Or they may be deep like mines, so that the chalk had to be raised by a windlass; and these are now protected by rails, and used only for depositing carrion. As a rule the bowl-shaped pits have been overgrown by bushes, or where large enough, planted with trees, with beech, oak, ash and holly; and they are surrounded by a hedge to keep out cattle. They have names of their own; often they are dells, such as Stubridge Dell, or Slade Dell. Thus they often form pretty little islands of copse in the middle of arable, and show their myriads of primroses or bluebells through the hazels when the neighbour field is crumbling dry in an east wind. These islands are attractive largely, I think, because they suggest fragments of primeval forest that have been left untouched by the plough on account of their roughness. I call them islands because that is the impression made on the passer-by. Cross over to them, and they are seen to be more like ponds full of everything but water. There are some small ones brimful of purple rosebay flowers in the midst of the corn. Others are full of all that a goldfinch loves – teasel, musk, thistle and sunshine. One is so broken up by the uneven diggings, the roots of trees, and the riot of brambles that a badger is safe in it with a whole pack of children. Some farms have one little or big dell to almost every field, and to enterprising children there must be large tracts of country which exist chiefly to provide these dells. One or two of the best of them are half-way between the hollow pit and the hill-side scoop. One in particular, a vast one, lies under a steep road which bends round it, and has to protect its passengers by posts and rails above the perpendicular. At the upper side it is precipitous, but it has a level floor, and the old entrance below is by a very gradual descent. It is very old, and some of the trees, which are now only butts, must have been two centuries old when they were felled. It is big enough for the Romany Rye to have fought there with the Flaming Tinman. But in Borrow's days it had more trees in it. Now it has about a score of tall ash trees only, ivy covered, and almost branchless, rising up out of it above the level of the road. Except at midsummer, only the tops of ash trees catch the sunlight. The rest is dark and wild, and somehow cruel. The woodmen looked tiny and dark, as if working for a punishment, when they were felling some of the trees below. The hundred yards or so of road running round the edge of the ancient pit is as fascinating as any other similar length in England. From the rails above you could well watch the Romany Rye and the Flaming Tinman and fair-haired Isopel.[24] But except the woodmen and the horses drawing out the timber, no one visits it. It is too gloomy. This is no vineyard, unless for growing the ruby grape of Proserpine, the nightshade. Though roofed with the sky, it has the effect of a cave, an entrance to the underworld.

Other roadside dells, facing the south or the southwest, are not so deserted. The old chalk pits, being too steep and rough to be cultivated, soon grow into places as wild as ancient Britain. They are especially good at a meeting of several roads. They form wayside wastes which are least easily enclosed. These strips are, or were, called slangs, and a waste of a larger kind gave us the curious word Flash. Flash is a village in a wild quarter of Derbyshire, between Buxton and Macclesfield. The people were mostly squatters who used the place as headquarters when they were not travelling to and from the fairs; and the lingo in which they talked to one another was called flash-talk. There is flash-talk still to be heard in some of the wayside chalk pits. There is no better place for a camp than one of these with a good aspect. It gives a man a little of the sense of a room. At the best it has almost four walls, which keep out neither sun nor rain. Some of them are much used by tramps and gypsies and other travellers.

[…]

It seems to require some philosophy to sit high on the Downs on a rainy February day, reading half a sheet of a week-old daily paper, on the leeside of a copse which was once a chalk pit. I have seen the man several times, but never observed that anyone was sitting at his feet to learn his wisdom. He had not wife, nor other possessions, nor desire to converse. He was lean, dirty, quite unpictur-esque and not strong, but he made quite the best of a wet February day. Most men would have preferred to be one of the chestnut horses ploughing near, their coats marked as with the hammer-marks on copper.

In summer, he and his kind are more picturesque. The best group I ever saw – and it was at the entrance to a chalk pit – was three wild women in black rags, with a perambu-lator and a large black cat. They had hair like hemp, and glittering blue eyes. They were lean but tall and strong. They were quite silent. When first I saw them they had a fire and were cooking – the cat knew what – upon a windy Sunday morning, while the church bells were ringing.

They were not supernatural, I can swear, because one of them asked the time as I left, though it was upon a solitary and remote roadway, and they appeared to have no affairs in this world that could depend upon 'the time'. I laughed at the question, and they seemed surprised, but they were too busy – thinking, shall I say? – to say any more. Two days later the races at __ began, but they were not there. On the morning of the races human beings crawled out of all kinds of holes, and the chalk puts supplied one or two. There is, presumably, no horse-racing after death, so that the lot of these devotees is not to be envied, though in this world they seem content. I saw one crawl out of an archway where a considerable stream of water ran in winter. But the chalk pit was better – it seemed to hold, as in a treasury, half the sun of a glorious morning, and across the floor, beside a dead fire, sprawled a middle-aged sportswoman in old black velvet, fast asleep, though the race-goers were streaming past in some haste. Those were the days of the green-finches – the little bands flitting and twittering through hedges and over yew trees with clear thin notes, breezy in the breeze – and of linnets scattering now over the brassy ragwort flowers, and millions of poppies in the wheat. Once I met a small bear in one of the tangled dells in this neighbourhood. He was curled up in the sun between bushes of gorse, and his master's head was buried in his fur. If the bear had been alone it might have been a scene in Britain before Caesar's time, but though it was 1904 the bear looked indigenous. This dell is one of those which may be natural or artificial, or perhaps partly both, a small natural coombe having been convenient for excavation of the chalk. It lies at the foot of a wild Down which is climbed chiefly for the sake of its chalk pits, by a slanting steep road. The dell is a long narrow chamber with a floor rising towards the beginning of the steep slope. The sides of it are worn by the rabbits and support little but gaunt elder bushes. The floor grows a few ash trees and much gorse. The tallest tree is dead, but the coombe is sheltered and the great ash still holds up its many arms in the form of a lyre, high above the rest. It is grey and stiff and without bark. But the jackdaws love it. All through the afternoons of summer they come and go among the hills, and the dead tree is their chief station. It might almost seem a religious place to them. There are always two or three perched on the topmost branches, talking to those arriving or departing. Now and then a turtledove flies up and they do not resent it. As to the bear, it was nothing to them. Their ancestors had seen many such. There are jackdaws in the elms of the neighbouring meadows, but those religious ones upon the dead ash tree seem the most important, and it alone is never deserted. ('Chalk Pits', *The Last Sheaf*, 27–37)

'The Chalk-Pit' (May 1915, *Last Poems*)

    'Is this the road that climbs above and bends
    Round what was once a chalk-pit: now it is
    By accident an amphitheatre.
    Some ash-trees standing ankle-deep in brier
    And bramble act the parts, and neither speak
    Nor stir.' 'But see: they have fallen, every one,
    And brier and bramble have grown over them.'
    'That is the place. As usual no one is here.
    Hardly can I imagine the drop of the axe,
    And the smack that is like an echo, sounding here.'
    'I do not understand.' 'Why, what I mean is
    That I have seen the place two or three times
    At most, and that its emptiness and silence
    And stillness haunt me, as if just before
    It was not empty, silent, still, but full
    Of life of some kind, perhaps tragical.
    Has anything unusual happened here?'
    'Not that I know of. It is called the Dell.
    They have not dug chalk here for a century.
    That was the ash-trees' age. But I will ask.'
    'No. Do not. I prefer to make a tale,

Or better leave it like the end of a play,
Actors and audience and lights all gone;
For so it looks now. In my memory
Again and again I see it, strangely dark,
And vacant of a life but just withdrawn.
We have not seen the woodman with the axe.
Some ghost has left it now as we two came.'
'And yet you doubted if this were the road?'
'Well, sometimes I have thought of it and failed
To place it. No. And I am not quite sure,
Even now, this is it. For another place,
Real or painted, may have combined with it.
Or I myself a long way back in time …'
'Why, as to that, I used to meet a man –
I had forgotten, – searching for birds' nests
Along the road and in the chalk-pit too.
The wren's hole was an eye that looked at him
For recognition. Every nest he knew.
He got a stiff neck, by looking this side or that,
Spring after spring, he told me, with his laugh, –
A sort of laugh. He was a visitor,
A man of forty, – smoked and strolled about.
At orts and crosses Pleasure and Pain had played
On his brown features; – I think both had lost; –
Mild and yet wild too. You may know the kind.
And once or twice a woman shared his walks,
A girl of twenty with a brown boy's face,
And hair brown as a thrush or as a nut,
Thick eyebrows, glinting eyes–' 'You have said
    enough.
A pair, – free thought, free love, – I know the breed:
I shall not mix my fancies up with them.'
'You please yourself. I should prefer the truth

Or nothing. Here, in fact, is nothing at all
Except a silent place that once rang loud,
And trees and us – imperfect friends, we men
And trees since time began; and nevertheless
Between us still we breed a mystery.'

The Landscape of the Imagination – Wales

The best way into Wales is the way you choose, provided that you care. Some may like the sudden modern way of going to sleep at London in a train and remaining asleep on a mountain-side, which has the advantage of being the most expensive and the least surprising way. Some may like to go softly into the land along the Severn, on foot, and going through sheath after sheath of the country, to reach at last the heart of it at peaty Tregaron, or the soul of it on Plynlimmon [Plynlimon] itself. Or you may go by train at night; and at dawn, on foot, follow a little stream at its own pace and live its fortnight's life from mountain to sea.

Or you may cross the Severn and then the lower Wye, and taking Tredegar and Caerleon alternately, or Rhigws [Rhigos] and Landore, or Cardiff and Llantwit [Llantwit], or the Rhondda Valley and the Vale of Neath, and thus sharpening the spirit, as an epicure may sharpen his palate, by opposites, find true Wales everywhere, whether the rivers be ochre and purple with corruption, or still as silver as the fountain dew on the mountain's beard; whether the complexions of the people be pure as those of the young cockle-women of Penclawdd, or as heavily superscribed as those of tin-platers preparing to wash. Or you may get no harm by treading in the footsteps of that warm-blooded antiquarian. Pennant, who wrote at the beginning of his tours in Wales:

'With obdurate valour we sustained our independency … against the power of a kingdom more than twelve times larger than Wales: and at length had the glory of falling, when a divided country, beneath the arms of the most wise and most warlike of the English monarchs'.[25] That 'we' may have saved the soul even of an antiquarian.

But the entry I best remember and most love was made by a child whom I used to know better than I have known anyone else. He disappeared, after a slow process of evanishment, several years ago: and I will use what I know as if it were my own, since the first person singular will help me to write as if I should never be subjected to the dignity of print, – as if I were addressing, not the general reader, but some one who cared.

At a very early age, I (that is to say, he, *bien entendu*) often sat in a room in outer London, where I now see that it was probably good to be. It was always October there, and the yellow poplar leaves were always falling. And so also there was always a fire – a casket in which emeralds and sapphires contended with darker spirits continually. Where are the poplars now? Where the leaves which loved the frost that spoiled them at last? Where the emeralds and sapphires – and the child? There were late October twilights that seemed so mighty in their gentleness and so terrible in their silence that they alarmed the child with fear of desolation, until the spell was suspended by lighted lamps and drawn curtains and fearless voices of elder persons, though one could draw the curtains and see the thing still, and oneself, and the very fire, outside in its embrace. And still

The jealous ear of night eave-dropped our talk.[26]

I think those twilights have overwhelmed all at last, and they have their way with child and trees and fire. But they have spared one thing, which even in those days was more puissant than the fire, though they have left their marks upon it, and now it seems a less mighty thing if one goes to it soberly too critically, or even too cheerfully. For a picture hung in the room, and the last October sunlight used to fall upon it when the silence set in. The picture meant Wales.

In the foreground, a stream shone with ripples in the midst, and glowed with foam among the roots of alders at the edge. Branches with white berries overhung the stream; and there were hornbeams and writhen oaks; and beyond them, a sky with a shaggy and ancient storm in it, and wrestling with that, and rising into it, the ruins of an Early English chancel. The strength and anger and tenderness and majesty of it, were one great thought I still think that could deeds spring panoplied from thoughts, and could great thoughts of themselves do anything but flush the cheek, such a simply curving landscape as this would be at the bidding of one of those great thoughts that empty all the brain … Under one of the columns by the chancel, the artist meant to have drawn vaguely a pile of masonry and a muscular ivy stem. And that was the point of the picture, because it seemed to be a kneeling knight, with one forearm on an oval shield and the other buried in his beard, and his head bent. I suppose that the thought that it was a knight, and that the knight was Launcelot, first came as I looked at the picture once, straight from a book where I had been reading:

'Then Sir Launcelot departed, and when he came to the Chapel Perilous, he alighted, and tied his horse to a little gate. And as soon as he was within the churchyard he saw on the front of the Chapel many fair, rich shields turned upside down; and many of the shields Sir Launcelot had seen knights have before; with that he saw standing by him thirty great knights, more by a yard than any man that he had ever seen, and all these grinned and gnashed at Sir Launcelot; and when he saw their countenances he dreaded them sore, and so put his shield afore him, and took his sword in his hand ready to do battle; and they were all armed in black harness, ready with their shields and swords drawn. And when Sir Launcelot would have gone through them they scattered on every side of him, and gave him the way to pass; and therewith he waxed all bold, and entered into the Chapel, and there he saw no light but a dim lamp burning, and then he was aware of a corse [*sic* – corpse] covered with a cloth of silk. And as Sir Launcelot stooped down and cut a piece of the cloth away, the earth quaked, and he was afraid ...'

And the picture was a picture of the Chapel Perilous; and thus out of a poor story-book and a dear picture and the dim poplars in the dim street, I made a Launcelot who was not merely an incredible medieval knight of flesh and armour, but a strange immortal figure that lived and was desirable and friendly in the grey rain of a suburb in the nineteenth century.

This was the beginning of the creation of Wales. Or shall I say that it was the beginning of the discovery? Let the reader decide, with the help of the explanation, that I use the words as I should use them of a play of Shakespeare's, or a picture of Titian's, or any other living thing which grows and changes and is born again, in age after age, as certainly and as elusively as the substance of a waterfall is changed; even in one moment these things are never the same to any two observers, backward or advanced, egotistical or servile, blind or keen ...

Looking back, the artistry of time makes it appear that soon after I had become certain that the painter had somehow caught Launcelot kneeling at the foot of the column, I reached Wales.

There I saw one of the Round Tables of Arthur, but also a porpoise hunt in the river close by; and the porpoise threshed the water so that the shining spray now hides the Round Table from my view. And I heard the national anthem of Wales: and at first I cowered beneath the resolved and terrible despair of it, forgetting that –

In every dirge there sleeps a battle-march;[27]

so that I seemed to look out from the folds of a fantastic purple curtain of heavily embroidered fabric upon a fair landscape and an awful sky; and I know not whether the landscape or the sky was the more fascinating in its mournfulness.

And I heard sounds of insult, shame, and wrong.

And trumpets blown for wars,[28]

– and it was of Arthur's last battle that I dreamed. But the sky cleared, and I seemed to let go of the folds of the curtain and to see a red dragon triumphing and the shielded Sir Launcelot again; and next, it was only a tournament that I saw, and there were careless ladies on high among the golden dust. And, at last, I could once more think happily of the little white house where I lived, and the largest and reddest apples in all the world that grew upon the wizened orchard, and the smoked salmon and the hams that perfumed the long kitchen, and all the shining candlesticks, and the wavy, crisp, thin leaves of oaten bread that were eaten there with buttermilk: and the great fire shook his rustling sheaf of flames and laughed at the wind and rain that stung the window-panes; and sometimes a sense of triumph arose from the glory of the fire and the vanity of the wind, and sometimes a sense of fear lest the fire should be conspiring with the storm. That also was Wales – a meandering village street, the house with the orchard, and a white river in sight of it, and the great music of the national anthem hovering over it and giving the whole a strange solemnity.

Just beyond the village, but not under the same solemn sky, I see an island of apple trees in spring, which in fact belongs to a somewhat later year. It was reached by a mile of winding lane that passed the slender outmost branches of the village, and lastly, a shining cottage, with streaked and mossy thatch, and two little six-paned windows, half-filled with many-coloured sweets, and boasting one pane of bottle-glass. Outside sat an old woman; her moist, grey, hempen curls framing a cruel face which had been made by three or four swift strokes of a hatchet; her magnificent brown eyes seeming to ponder heavenly things and really looking for half-pence. A picture would have made her – wringing her hands slowly as if she were perpetually washing, or sitting bolt upright and pleased with her white apron – a type of resigned and reverend and beautiful old age. On the opposite side of the road was a white and thatched piggery, half the size of the house; and along-side of it, a neat, moulded pile of coal-dust, clay, and lime, mixed, for her ever-burning fire. The pigs grunted; the old woman, who would herself watch the slaughtering, sat and was pleased and said, 'Good morning,' and 'Good afternoon,' and 'Good evening' as the day went by, except when the children were due to pass to and from school, with half-pence to spend.

Just beyond this dragon and its house, an important road crossed the lane, which then narrowed and allowed the hedgerow hazels to arch over it and let in only the wannest light to the steep, stony hedge-bank of whin[29] and grass and fern and violets. Little streams ran this way and that, under and over and alongside the lane, and at length a larger one was honoured by a bridge, the parapet covered with flat, dense, even turf. The bridge made way for a wide view, and to invite the eye a magpie flew away from the grassy parapet with wavy flight to a mountain side.

Between the bridge and the mountain, and in fact surrounded by streams which were heard although unseen, was an island of apple trees.

There were murmurs of bees. There was a gush and fall and gurgle of streams, which could be traced by their bowing irises. There was a poignant glow and fragrance of flowers in an air so moist and cold and still that at dawn the earliest bee left a thin line of scent upon it Beyond, the mountain, grim, without trees, lofty and dark, was clearly upholding the low blue sky full of slow clouds of the colour of the mountain lambs or of melting snow. This mountain and this sky, for that first hour, shut out, and not only shut out but destroyed, and not only destroyed but made as if it had never been, the world of the old woman, the coal-pits, the schools, and the grown-up persons. And the magic of Wales, or of Spring, or of childhood made the island of apple trees more than an orchard in flower. For as some women seem at first to be but rich eyes in a mist of complexion and sweet voice, so the orchard was but an invisible soul playing with scent and colour as symbols. Nor did this wonder vanish when I walked among the trees and looked up at the blossoms in the sky. For in that island of apple trees there was not one tree but was curved and jagged and twisted and splintered by great age, by the west wind, or by the weight of fruit in many autumns. In colour they were stony. They were scarred with knots like mouths. Some of their branches were bent sharply like lightning flashes. Some rose up like bony, sunburnt, imprecating arms of furious prophets. One stiff, gaunt bole that was half hid in flower might have been Ares' sword in the hands of the Cupids. Others were like ribs of submerged ships, or the horns of an ox emerging from a skeleton deep in the sand of a lonely coast. And the blossom of them all was the same, so that they seemed to be Winter with the frail Spring in his arms. Nor was I surprised when the first cuckoo sang therein, since the blossom made it for its need. And when a curlew called from the mountain hopelessly, I laughed at it.

When I came again and saw the apple trees in flower, the island was very far away, and the unseen cuckoo sang behind a veil and not so suitably as the curlew. There was something of the dawn in the light over it, though it was midday; and I could hardly understand, and was inclined to melancholy, until chance brought into my head the poem of the old princely warrior poet Llywarch Hên, and out of his melancholy and mine was born a mild and lasting joy.[30] He sang:

> Sitting high upon a hill, to battle is inclined
> My mind, but it does not impel me onward.
> Short is my journey my tenement is laid waste.
>
> Sharp is the gale, it is bare punishment to live.
> When the trees array themselves in gay colours
> Of Summer, extremely ill am I this day.
>
> I am no hunter, I keep no animal of the chase,
> I cannot move about:
> As long as it pleases the cuckoo, let her sing.
>
> The loud-voiced cuckoo sings with the dawn,
> Her melodious notes in the dales of Cuawg:
> Better than the miser is the lavish man.

At Aber Cuawg the cuckoos sing.
On the blossom-covered branches;
Woe to the sick that hears their contented notes.

At Aber Cuawg the cuckoos sing.
The recollection is in my mind.
There are that hear them that will not hear them
    again.

Have I not listened to the cuckoo on the ivied tree?
Did not my shield hang down?
What I loved is but vexation; what I loved is no
    more.

And I thought that perhaps it is even true, as Taliesin sang, that 'A man is wont to be oldest when born, and younger all the time,' and that the apple flowers did but remind me of old capacities laid waste. These little things are the opening cadences of a great music which I have heard, and which is Wales. But I have forgotten the whole, and have echoes of it only, when I hear an old Welsh song, when I am trying to catch a trout, or am eating bread and butter and white cheese, and drinking pale tea, in a mountain farm ... One echo of it I had strangely in Oxford, when, entertaining an old wise gipsy, and asking him of his travels, and whether he had been in Wales, he meditated for a long time, and then sang in an emotionless and moving tone the 'Hen wlad fy nhadau,'[31] up there among the books, the towers, and the stars. I have had a vision of a rose. But my memory possesses only the doubtful and withered dustiness of a petal or two. (*Beautiful Wales,* 1905, 28–40)

Southern England – 'The Brook' (July 1915 from *Last Poems*)

Seated once by a brook, watching a child
Chiefly that paddled, I was thus beguiled.
Mellow the blackbird sang and sharp the thrush
Not far off in the oak and hazel brush,
Unseen. There was a scent like honeycomb
From mugwort dull. And down upon the dome
Of the stone the cart-horse kicks against so oft
A butterfly alighted. From aloft
He took the heat of the sun, and from below.
On the hot stone he perched contented so,
As if never a cart would pass again
That way; as if I were the last of men
And he the first of insects to have earth
And sun together and to know their worth.
I was divided between him and the gleam,
The motion, and the voices, of the stream,
The waters running frizzled over gravel,
That never vanish and for ever travel.
A grey flycatcher silent on a fence
And I sat as if we had been there since
The horseman and the horse lying beneath
The fir-tree-covered barrow on the heath,
The horseman and the horse with silver shoes,
Galloped the downs last. All that I could lose
I lost. And then the child's voice raised the dead.
'No one's been here before' was what she said
And what I felt, yet never should have found
A word for, while I gathered sight and sound.

23 Bracken or brake fern (*Pteridium aquilinum*).

24 From George Borrow's autobiographical work *Romany Rye*, 1857.

25 Thomas Pennant, *A Tour in Wales*, 1778.

26 *Antonio and Mellida,* by John Marston, circa 1599.

27 Ernest Rhys, 'Envoi'.

28 Tennyson, 'A Dream of Fair Women'.

29 'Whin' – gorse.

30 Llywarch the Old is a sixth-century prince and bard to whom a series of poetic cycles in the Red Book of Hergest are attributed, including this one, which is called 'Sitting high upon a hill'. It is believed that Aber Cuawg is an early name for the mouth of the River Dulas, near Machynlleth.

31 'Old Land of My Fathers', the Welsh national anthem.

Chapter Five

The Journey

Edward Thomas's journeys were as much mental as they were physical. We will see Thomas planning his journey westward for his 1913 book *In Pursuit of Spring* to observe the birth of spring during a 'March Easter', to Kilve, in Somerset, from London, imagining the various trajectories. Once he reached the coast he added an extra loop inland to Cothelstone Hill, in Somerset, to observe both 'winter's grave' and a view of the hills of Wales. We often don't know why exactly Thomas chose to visit the places he did in his travel books, although he was less attached to physical challenge or cultural significance than to subconscious urges.

In the journey described in *In Pursuit of Spring* Thomas cycled and walked with companions but this wasn't stated – instead we hear about the associations with earlier writers: Stephen Duck, William Cowper, Philip Sidney, George Bourne (author of *The Bettesworth Book*), W.H. Hudson, Thomas Hardy, William Barnes, William Cobbett, and Samuel Taylor Coleridge, among others. Yet he was interested in the landmarks of everyday people – including weathercocks, epitaphs, monuments, advertisements, inns and houses. What excited him most were the unexpected encounters with people, beauty, weather and wildlife on route. And as he met others, including the fictitious 'Other Man' described in the following chapter, we see the narrator analysing himself and grappling with the depression that had plagued the author since *The Icknield Way* (which was written in 1911 but published in 1913).

The Icknield Way follows the Neolithic route (or network of routes) which connected the flint-mining people of Thetford in East Anglia to the inhabitants of what is now Wiltshire, along a belt of turf along the chalk ridge that avoided the marshes and forest (but not high enough to be on the skyline). Unlike the higher Ridgeway (or Great Ridgeway), with which it interweaves and eventually seems to merge towards the south-west, the Icknield Way is not a way-marked National Trail, so it still offers a modern walker some of the mystery that it held for Thomas. While many ancient trackways will have become roads, the long-distance nature of these two paths meant they often outlived paths that connected modern settlements. And yet there are still disputes as to the exact routes (as Thomas noted in *The Icknield Way*). This chapter also includes a few quotation relating to the practicalities of long-distance walking, as well as Thomas's reflections on pilgrimage.

Setting out – Choosing a Route

That evening, without thought of Spring, I began to look at my maps. Spring would come, of course – nothing, I supposed, could prevent it – and I should have to make up my mind how to go westward. Whatever I did, Salisbury Plain was to be crossed, not of necessity but of choice; it was, however, hard to decide whether to go reasonably diagonally in accordance with my western purpose, or to meander up the Avon, now on one side now on the other, by one of the parallel river-side roads, as far as Amesbury. Having got to Amesbury, there would be much provocation to continue up the river among those thatched villages to Upavon and to Stephen Duck's village, Charlton, and the Pewsey valley, and so, turning again westward, in sight of that very tame White Horse above Alton Priors,[32] to include Urchfont and Devizes.

Or, again, I might follow up the Wylye westward from Salisbury, and have always below me the river and its hamlets and churches, the wall of the Plain always above me on the right. Thus I should come to Warminster and to the grand west wall of the Plain which overhangs the town.

The obvious way was to strike north-west over the Plain from Stapleford up the Winterbourne, through cornland and sheepland, by Shrewton and Tilshead, and down again to other waters at West Lavington. Or at Shrewton I could turn sharp to the west, and so visit solitary Chitterne and solitary Imber.

I could not decide. If I went on foot, I could do as I liked on the Plain. There are green roads leading from everywhere to everywhere. But, on the other hand, it might be necessary at that time of year to keep walking all day, which would mean at least thirty miles a day, which was more than I was inclined for. (*In Pursuit of Spring*, 1914, 15–16)

'The Avon, the Biss, the Frome' – Walking and Cycling

Once in the night I awoke and heard the weir again, but the first sound in the morning was a thrush singing in a lilac next my window. For the main chorus of dawn was over. It was a still morning under a sky that was one low arch of cloud, a little whiter in places, but all grey. Big drops glistened on the undersides of horizontal rails. There had been a white frost, and, as they said, we seldom have many white frosts before it rains again. But not until I went out could I tell that it was softly and coldly raining. Everything more than two or three fields away was hidden.

Cycling is inferior to walking in this weather, because in cycling chiefly ample views are to be seen, and the mist conceals them. You travel too quickly to notice many small things; you see nothing save the troops of elms on the verge of invisibility. But walking I saw every small thing one by one; not only the handsome gateway chestnut just fully dressed, and the pale green larch plantation where another chiff-chaff was singing, and the tall elm tipped by a linnet pausing and musing a few notes, but every primrose and celandine and dandelion on the banks, every silvered green leaf of honeysuckle up in the hedge, every patch of brightest moss, every luminous drop on a thorn tip. The world seemed a small place: as I went between a row of elms and a row of beeches occupied by rooks, I had a feeling that the road, that the world itself, was private, all theirs; and the state of the road under their nests confirmed me. I was going hither and thither today in the neighbourhood of my stopping place, instead of continuing my journey. (*In Pursuit of Spring*, 199–200)

'Early one morning' (June 1916, *Poems*)

Early one morning in May I set out,
And nobody I knew was about.
　　I'm bound away for ever,
　　Away somewhere, away for ever.

There was no wind to trouble the weathercocks.
I had burnt my letters and darned my socks.

No one knew I was going away,
I thought myself I should come back some day.

I heard the brook through the town gardens run.
O sweet was the mud turned to dust by the sun.

A gate banged in a fence and banged in my head.
'A fine morning, sir,' a shepherd said.

I could not return from my liberty,
To my youth and my love and my misery.

The past is the only dead thing that smells sweet,
The only sweet thing that is not also fleet.
 I'm bound away for ever,
 Away somewhere, away for ever.

'Over the Hills' (January 1915, *Last Poems*)

Often and often it came back again
To mind, the day I passed the horizon ridge
To a new country, the path I had to find
By half-gaps that were stiles once in the hedge,
The pack of scarlet clouds running across
The harvest evening that seemed endless then
And after, and the inn where all were kind,
All were strangers. I did not know my loss
Till one day twelve months later suddenly
I leaned upon my spade and saw it all,
Though far beyond the sky-line. It became
Almost a habit through the year for me

To lean and see it and think to do the same
Again for two days and a night. Recall
Was vain: no more could the restless brook
Ever turn back and climb the waterfall
To the lake that rests and stirs not in its nook,
As in the hollow of the collar-bone
Under the mountain's head of rush and stone.

Nowhere to Stay – Chiseldon, Wiltshire

I was hungry when I knocked at the door of the first inn at half-past five. On the opposite side of the road a small, quiet crowd of drinkers in black coats and hats waited to be let in at six. No one answered my knock. I knocked louder, and still louder, on the woodwork of the door. Then I rapped the glass, and rapped louder and many times. But no one came, and as I was too hungry to want justice I went to the next inn. Here the door was instantly opened by a little red-faced landlady with fuzzy hair and a gnomish face. She was swift and clean, and so light and quick was her step that every time I heard her approaching I expected a child. She was sorry to say that she had no bed to spare, but told me of someone that might. I tried in vain, then called opposite where 'refreshments' were advertised. An enormous woman stood wedged in the doorway; she was black-haired, sullen, and faintly moustached, and she had her hands hanging down because there was no room on either side of her to clasp them, and no room in the doorway for her to rest them upon the fat superincumbent upon her hips. I said good evening, and she remained silent. I asked her if she had a bed to spare. She looked me up and down with a movement of head and eyes, and asked me gradually where I came from. I was so taken aback that

I told her like a child, 'From East Hendred' – which was absurd. She retreated to ask her husband. He appeared alone, and hanging down his head, shook it, and said that he did not think he could spare me a bed. Having no gift of speech, I turned very rapidly away from him and back to the inn. The landlady thought of someone else, made inquiries, and assured me that the bed would be ready when Mrs. Somebody got back from church. So I went out and looked at Burderop, Ladder Hill, and the turning 'To the Downs and Rockley'. The woman was back from church and opened the door to me. She had a background of women taking off Sunday hats and putting away veils and prayer-books, and said she was sorry, but a niece had come, and there was no room for me. In the darkening street I saw an old man at a gate with a genial face and the mouth of one accustomed to horses. I asked him if he knew of a bed to spare. 'No – oh-oh-oh – no,' he chuckled, with increased geniality. 'You've come to the wrong place … Oh-ho-ho-ho-ho no,' he continued. 'I can't tell you why; but if you want a bed you have to go to a town'. He was only a visitor to Chisledon [*sic* – Chiseldon], and I wished him better treatment than I had got. I set out for Swindon. In about a mile I came to another inn, where I had always enjoyed the bread and cheese and ale, and I unwillingly silenced a black-coated company of grave drinkers standing at the bar. They suspended their glasses while the landlord said that it was absolutely impossible to get a bed that side of Swindon. I tried at Coate. The barmaid appealed to Mr. MacFaggart, who was standing by – 'Perhaps Mrs. MacFaggart can spare a bed? ' 'No.' This series of refusals was, I am convinced, pure ill-luck. But the stout woman refused me, almost beyond doubt, because I was a stranger whom she could not immediately classify. I could not be classed as a 'gentleman', as a young 'gent' or 'swell', or as a plain 'young fellow'. She decided not to risk it. Perhaps she had savings about the house. Or did she think that underneath less than two days' beard, that oldish and not very clean Burberry waterproof, those good but very baggy trousers, murder was lurking? No, probably she felt not the very slightest inclination to please me, and as it only meant half a crown, her one difficulty in refusing was her natural sullenness increased by the presence of the nondescript and unsympathetic casual stranger on a Sunday. Country people know a country gentleman, a sporting financier, a tradesman, a young townsman (clerk or artisan), a working man, and a real tramp or roadster. Some of them know the artist or distinguished foreigner, with a foot of hair, broad-brimmed hat, and corduroy or soft tweeds, a cloak and an ostentatious pipe, tasselled, or of enormous bulk, or elaborate form or unusual substance. Some know the hairy and hygienic man in sandals. To be elbowed out at night-fall after a day's walking by an unconscious conspiracy of a whole village was enough to produce either a hate of Chisledon or a belief that the devil or a distinguished relative was organizing the opposition. But during those four unexpected miles to Swindon in the volcanic heat of evening, which produced several pains and a constant struggle between impatient mind and dull, tired body, I felt chiefly: I suffer; I do not want to suffer; and only now and then the face of Mrs. Stout, or of Mrs. Smallbeer, or of the genial old man with the horsy mouth, came into my head, and turned my depression to fury.

Possibly they were afraid of German spies at Chisledon. Not far from Maidstone in the summer of 1910 some poor cottage children were telling me how a German spy wanted to rob them of the lunch they were taking to school. He was a dark stranger with a beard, and he was waiting about at a crossing partly overhung by trees; and they were convinced that he wished to steal their food, and that his reason for doing so was his position as German spy.

At Swindon I felt what a man feels in a place where he knows one man instead of knowing scores of children and feeling that every passing stranger was of the same family, ready at a touch to be changed to a friend. But I had no difficulty in finding a bed surrounded by the following decorations: pictures of ships in quiet and in roaring seas; of roses twining about the words, 'The Lord shall be thy everlasting light'; of a cart-horse going through a ford with three children on his back; of an Italian boatman and three buxom girls, one clinking glasses with him; advertisements of an aperient and of cheap cigarettes. The advertisement of cigarettes dwarfed all the rest. For not only was the lettering large, but there was also a coloured picture of a swarthy and hearty woman practically naked to the waist. She was smiling with her dark eyes, and her lips were parted. I could not imagine what she had to do with cigarettes of any kind. Was there a kind of suggestion that these bold, bad, under-dressed foreign beauties – undoubtedly beauties – were capable of smoking the cigarettes? Or was the picture meant to be a stimulus to some, a satisfaction to others, of those who sat at their ease drinking and smoking and thinking of women? In the tap-room of the most rustic public houses two or three of these women sometimes adorn the walls, along with a picture of a diseased cow and of its mouth, stomach, and udder. Some are dark, some are fair, and, I think, certainly meant to be English; but all are incompletely draped and unashamed. The dark ones are vaunting heathen beauties, the fair tend to be insipid, with expressions borrowed from the pious virgins of religious pictures. Sometimes the Bacchante and the pious virgin are to be seen side by side, the sacred one being supplied by the village grocer at Christmas. They are equally beautiful, i.e. have regular features, perfect complexions, and expressionless mouths, and are doing nothing in particular except posing so that the artist shall observe their bosoms, or, in the case of sacred pictures, their throats and the whites of their eyes. I do not think it could be shown that these pictures spoil the chances of girls with unclassical features and cross-eyes in the villages. In these matters the moth that desires the star is likely to end in a candle flame, whether or not he mistook it for a star. In these new towns I see women looking as if they were made in the chemists' shops, which are so numerous and conspicuous in the streets — thin, pallid, dyspeptic, vampirine beauties, having nothing but sex in common with the bold, swarthy alien on the cigarette advertisement ...

At Swindon the explorer of the Icknield Way has all the world before him. He may go through Marlborough into the Pewsey Valley, and either along under the hills through Lavington to Westbury, or, turning out of the Pewsey Valley, to Old Sarum, and beyond Westbury or Sarum into the extreme west; and he will be on a road of the same type as the Icknield Way for the greater part of the distance. Or he may content himself with reaching Avebury. Or he may miss Avebury and aim at Bath. At present documents and traditions keep a perfect silence west of Wanborough, and among mere possibilities the choice is endless. (*The Icknield Way*, 1913, 304–10).

'The Owl' (February 1915, *Poems*)

> Downhill I came, hungry, and yet not starved;
> Cold, yet had heat within me that was proof
> Against the North wind; tired, yet so that rest
> Had seemed the sweetest thing under a roof.
>
> Then at the inn I had food, fire, and rest,
> Knowing how hungry, cold, and tired was I.
> All of the night was quite barred out except
> An owl's cry, a most melancholy cry
>
> Shaken out long and clear upon the hill,
> No merry note, nor cause of merriment,
> But one telling me plain what I escaped
> And others could not, that night, as in I went.
>
> And salted was my food, and my repose,
> Salted and sobered, too, by the bird's voice
> Speaking for all who lay under the stars,
> Soldiers and poor, unable to rejoice.

Pilgrimage – Over Salisbury Plain

The Winterbourne guides you through the heart of the Plain. It has, I believe, no very strict boundaries, but the Plain may be said to consist of all that mass of downland in South Wiltshire, which is broken only by the comparatively narrow valleys of five rivers – the Bourne, the Avon, the Wylye, the Nadder, and the Ebble. Three of these valleys, however, those of the Bourn on the east, and of the Wylye and the Nadder on the south, have railways in them as well as rivers. The railways are more serious interruptions to the character of the Plain, and whether or not they must be regarded as the boundaries of a reduced Plain, certainly the core of the Plain excludes them. Even so it has to admit the Amesbury and Military Camp Light Railway, cutting across from the Bourn to the Avon, and there ceasing. Within this reduced space of fifteen by twenty miles the Plain is nothing but the Plain. As for the military camps, nothing may be seen of them for days beyond the white tents gleaming in the sun like sheep or clouds. When they are out of sight the tumuli and ancient earthworks that abound bring to mind more forcibly than anywhere else the fact that, as the poet says, 'the dead are more numerous than the living'.[33]

The valleys are rivers not only of waters, but of greenest grass and foliage. The greatest part of the Plain is all treeless pasture, treeless arable land. Some high places, as at meetings of roads, possess beeches or fir trees in line or cluster. Where the ground falls too steeply for cultivation a copse has been formed – a copse in one case, between Shrewton and Tilshead, of beautiful contour, following the steep wall of chalk for a quarter of a mile in a crescent curve, with level green at its foot, the high Down rising bare above it. A space here and there has been left to thorns and gorse bushes. In several places, as at Asserton Farm above Berwick St. James, plantations have been made in mathematical forms. But as you travel across the Plain you come rarely to a spot where the chief thing for the eye is not an immense expanse of the colour of ploughed chalk-land, or of corn, or of turf, varying according to season and weather, and always diversified by parallelograms of mustard yellow. Sometimes this expanse rolls but little before it touches the horizon; far more often, it heaves or billows up boldly into several long curving ridges that intersect or flow into one another. The highest of these may be crowned by dark beeches or carved by the ditch and rampart of an ancient camp. Hedges are few, even by the roads. The roads are among the noblest, visiting the rivers and their orchards and thatched villages, but keeping for the main part of their length high and dry and in long curves. They are travelled by an occasional (but not sufficiently occasional) motor car, or by a homeward going farm-roller with children riding the horses.

Next to the dead the most numerous things on the Plain are sheep, rooks, pewits, and larks. Today they mingle their voices, but the lark is the most constant. Here, more than elsewhere, he rises up above an earth only less free than the heavens. The pewit is equally characteristic. His Winter and twilight cry expresses for most men both the sadness and the wildness of these solitudes. When his Spring cry breaks every now and then, as it does today, through the songs of the larks, when the rooks caw in low flight or perched on their elm tops, and the lambs bleat, and the sun shines, and the couch fires burn well, and the wind blows their smoke about, the Plain is genial, and the unkindly breadth and simplicity of the scene in Winter or in the drought of Summer are forgotten. But let the rain fall and the wind whirl it, or let the sun shine too mightily, the Plain assumes the character by which it is best known, that of a sublime, inhospitable wilderness. It makes us feel the age of the earth, the greatness of Time, Space, and Nature; the little-ness of man even in an aeroplane, the fact that the earth does not belong to man, but man to the earth. And this feeling, or some variety of it, for most men is accompanied by melancholy, or is held to be the same thing. This is perhaps particularly so with townsmen, and above all with writers, because melancholy is the mood most easily given an appearance of profundity, and, therefore, most easily impressive. (*In Pursuit of Spring*, 147–50)

'The Child in the Orchard' (October 1916, *Last Poems*)

> 'He rolls in the orchard: he is stained with moss
> And with earth, the solitary old white horse.
> Where is his father and where is his mother
> Among all the brown horses? Has he a brother?
> I know the swallow, the hawk, and the hern;
> But there are two million things for me to learn.
>
> 'Who was the lady that rode the white horse
> With rings and bells to Banbury Cross?
> Was there no other lady in England beside
> That a nursery rhyme could take for a ride?
> The swift, the swallow, the hawk, and the hern.
> There are two million things for me to learn.
> '
> 'Was there a man once who straddled across
> The back of the Westbury White Horse
> Over there on Salisbury Plain's green wall?
> Was he bound for Westbury, or had he a fall?
> The swift, the swallow, the hawk, and the hern.
> There are two million things for me to learn.
>
> 'Out of all the white horses I know three,
> At the age of six; and it seems to me
> There is so much to learn, for men,
> That I dare not go to bed again.
> The swift, the swallow, the hawk, and the hern.
> There are millions of things for me to learn.'

'The Pilgrim' in *The Last Sheaf*

The 'Dark Lane' is the final half-mile of a Pilgrims' Way to St David's. It may be seen turning out of the Cardiganshire coast road a little north of the city. Presently it crosses the 'Roman road' to Whitesand Bay, and then goes down into the little quiet valley that holds the cathedral and a farm and a mill or two. Travel has hollowed out this descent; bramble and furze bushes on the banks help to darken it. Yet the name of 'Dark Lane' is due rather to the sense of its ancientness than to an extremity of shade. Perhaps on account of the shadow it may cast on the spirits of men it is now little used, unless by the winter rains; and some days of storm had made it more a river than a road when I walked it, away from St. David's. I looked back once or twice at the valley, its brook – the Alan – its cathedral, and the geese on its rushy and stony pasture. I had no conscious thought of antiquity, or of anything older than the wet green money-wort leaves on the stone of the banks beside me, or the points of gorse blossom, or a jackdaw's laughter in the keen air. If the pilgrims never entered my mind, neither did living people. The lane itself, just for what it was, absorbed and quieted me.

I was therefore disturbed when suddenly, among the gorse bushes, I saw a young man kneeling on the ground, his back turned towards me. If he had not heard me approaching he knew, as soon as I stopped, that someone was there. He was more surprised and far more disturbed than I. For in a flash I had seen what he was kneeling for; and he knew it. He was cutting a cross on a piece of rock which had been left uncovered by money-wort. Obviously he felt that I must think it odd employment for him on that December day.

He was not a workman carving a sign or a boundary stone, or anything of that sort. He was nothing like a workman, but was clearly a young man on a walk. A knapsack and a thick stick lay at his side. He was dressed in clothes of a rough homespun, dark sandy in colour, good, and the better for wear, and with nothing remarkable about them except that the coat was not divided and buttoned down the front, but was made to put on over his head. As he wore breeches he showed a sufficient pair of rather long legs. His head was bare, and his brown hair was untidy, and longer than is considered necessary for whatever purposes hair may be supposed to serve. He might have been twenty-five, and I put him down as perhaps a poet of a kind, who made a living out of prose.

He looked at me with his proud, helpless, blue eyes; his lips moving with unspoken words. He shut the knife he had been using as a chisel, and opened it again. I knew that he would have given anything for me to go on after saying 'Good morning,' but I did not go. I asked him how far it was to Llanrhian, and if the main road beyond here was the original continuation of the 'Dark Lane,' or if part of it was missing, and so on. He answered, probably, by no means as best he could, for he was thinking hard about himself. In a few minutes he could no longer keep himself to himself, but began to talk.

'I suppose you wonder what I was doing, cutting that cross?' he said in a defensive tone.

'Was there an old pilgrim's cross there?' I asked innocently. 'I have heard they carved crosses on some of the stones along the road.'

'I have heard so too,' he said; 'but I have been looking out for them all the way from Cardigan and I have not found any.'

'Then you have carved this yourself?'

'Yes; and I suppose you wonder why. Well, I don't know; I can't tell you; I don't suppose you would understand; I am not sure if I do myself; and at any rate it is no good now.'

'I hope my interrupting you …'

'Oh, no, I don't think so. But when I began I thought it would be a good thing. I got as far as this at daybreak, and I was feeling … what is it you? Seeing this old stone, which is perhaps the last before I reach the cathedral, and no cross on it any more than on the others, an idea came to me. I had been thinking about those pilgrims, some of them with torn feet, some hungry, or old, or friendless, or with an incurable disease. And yet they came here to St. David's shrine. They must have thought there was some good in doing so; they would be better, even though their feet might still be torn, or they might still be old, or hungry, or friendless, or have their incurable disease. But the shrine is now empty. I did think that perhaps the place where the relics used to be, when they were not carried out to battle, would have some power. All that faith would have given it some quality above common stone. But I doubted. Then I thought. 'But faith is the thing. If those pilgrims had faith there was no special good in St. David's bones, except, again, that they believed there was.' I tried to think in what spirit one of them would have carved a cross. Perhaps just as a boy cuts his name or whatever it may be on a bridge, thinking about anything or nothing all the time, or sucking a pebble to quench his thirst. At the sight of this stone – I may have been a fool – I thought – I had the feeling that while I was doing as the pilgrims did I might become like one of them. So I threw off my knapsack and chiselled away… 'Please don't apologise. In any case it would have been no good. The knife was already too blunt, and I was cold and aching and also thinking of a wretched poem. Do you think a pilgrim ever had such thoughts? If there was such a one he would never have got far on his road.'

I tried hard to lure him into a Socratic dialogue to disclose what had brought him so far. He went on:

'The quickest city in the world is St. Pierre, which was overwhelmed by the volcano on Mont Pelée. But one cannot easily become a citizen of St. Pierre. Well, well, what is it to you that I want in some way to be better than I am? I must be born again: that is certain. So far as it is in my power, I have tried hard. For example, there is no ordinary food or drink or article of clothing I have not given up at some time, and no extraordinary one that I have not adopted. There remains only to wear a silk hat and to drink beer for breakfast.

'I have been to physicians, surgeons, and enchanters, but they all want to know what is the matter with me. I answer that I came to them to find out. Then they listen gravely while I tell them about a hundredth part of the outline of my life. They write out prescriptions; they order me to eat more or less, or to be very careful in every way, or not to worry about anything. They shake hands, saying: "I was just like you when I was your age. You will be all right before long. Good-bye".

'My family once paid a specialist to come to see me at the house once. He and I had the usual conversation. Then he was given lunch, which he ate in complete silence, except for a complaint about the steak. After receiving his cheque my mother asked him rather tragically what to do. "Don't hurry him on, Mrs. Jones," he said, "and don't keep him back, Mrs. Jones".

'For forty days I visited an enchanter continually. He did not promise to cure me, though he also said that at my age he was just like me – which was untrue, for he had a Yorkshire accent. Day after day in his room I say with closed eyes, repeating "Lycidas," silently with the object of not thinking about anything, especially the incantation. This consisted of a whispered, slightly hesitating assertion that I should get well, that I should be happy, that I should faith, that I should have no more doubt, but confidence, concentration, self-control, and good sleep. After several minutes I always heard the enchanter take out his watch to see if he had given me enough. From that time until the end I was doing little but listening to the crackle of his shirt-front and cuffs. It was so funny that I was even more serious about it than he; but after forty days I had had enough. My rebirth did not take place in the house of the enchanter.'

'When I was your age …' I began; but luckily I was inaudible.

'I have tried many medicines,' he continued. 'I have been to a physician who offers to cure men who are suffering from many medicines. All in vain. I tried a medicine which all great writers take, and which presumably makes them greater or keeps them great; but it had no effect on me – my literary ambition died.'

Here he took out his watch.

'Zeus!' he said. 'I have been two hours at this thing,' and he rose up. 'I must photograph that cross and put it in my book. That will pay for the wasted time.'

He photographed the stone and cross, and departed with long strides down the 'Dark Lane' before I could ask about his book, but I see no reason to doubt that he was writing a book. (*The Last Sheaf*, 1928, 51–58)

The Stile

Three roads meet in the midst of a little green without a house or the sign of one, and at one edge there is an oak copse with untrimmed hedges. One road goes east, another west, and the other north; southward goes a path known chiefly to lovers, and the stile which transfers them to it from the rushy turf is at a corner of the copse.

The country is low, rich in grass and small streams, mazily sub-divided by crooked hedgerows, with here and there tall oaks in broken lines or, round the farm houses, in musing protective clusters. It is walled in by hills on every side, the higher ones bare, the lower furred with trees, and so nearly level is it that, from any part of it, all these walls of hills, and their attendant clouds can be seen.

I have known the copse well for years. It holds an acre of oaks two or three generations old, the roots of ancient ones, and an undergrowth of hazel and brier which is nearly hidden by the high thorn hedge.

One day I stopped by the stile at the corner to say good-bye to a friend who had walked thus far with me. It was about half an hour after the sunset of a dry, hot day among the many wet ones in that July. We had been talking easily and warmly together, in such a way that there was no knowing whose was any one thought, because we were in electrical contact and each leapt to complete the other's words, just as if some poet had chosen to use the form of an eclogue and had made us the two shepherds who were to utter his mind through our dialogue. When he spoke I had already the same thing in the same words to express. When either of us spoke we were saying what we could not have said to any other man at any other time.

But as we reached the stile our tongues and our steps ceased together, and I was instantly aware of the silence through which our walking and talking had drawn a thin line up to this point. We had been going on without looking at one another in the twilight. Now we were face to face. We wished to go on speaking but could not. My eyes wandered to the rippled outline of the dark heavy hills against the sky, which was now pale and barred with the grey ribs of a delicate sunset. High up I saw Gemma;[34] I even began trying to make out the bent star bow of which it is the centre. I saw the plain, now a vague dark sea of trees and hedges, where lay my homeward path. Again I looked at the face near me, and one of us said:

'The weather looks a little more settled'.
The other replied: 'I think it does.'

I bent my head and tapped the toe of my shoe with my stick, wishing to speak, wishing to go, but aware of a strong unknown power which made speech impossible and yet was not violent enough to detach me altogether and at once from the man standing there. Again my gaze wandered dallying to the hills – to the sky and the increase of stars – the darkness of the next hedge – the rushy green, the pale roads and the faint thicket mist that was starred with glow-worms. The scent of the honeysuckles and all those hedges was in the moist air. Now and then a few unexpected, startled and startling words were spoken, and the silence drank them up as the sea drinks a few tears. But always my roving eyes returned from the sky, the hills, the plain to those other greenish eyes in the dusk, and then with a growing sense of rest and love to the copse waiting there, its indefinite cloud of leaves and branches and, above that, the outline of oak tops against the sky.

It was very near. It was still, sombre, silent. It was vague and unfamiliar. I had forgotten that it was a copse and one that I had often seen before. White roses like mouths penetrated the mass of the hedge.

I found myself saying 'good-bye'. I heard the word 'good-bye' spoken. It was a signal not of a parting but of a uniting. In spite of the unwillingness to be silent with my friend a moment before, a deep ease and confidence was mine underneath that unrest. I took one or two steps to the stile and, instead of crossing it I leaned upon the gate at one side. The confidence and ease deepened and darkened as if I also were like that still, sombre cloud that had been a copse, under the pale sky that was light without shedding light. I did not disturb the dark rest and beauty of the earth which had ceased to be ponderous, hard matter and had become itself cloudy or, as it is when the mind thinks of it, spiritual stuff, so that the glow-worms shone through it as stars through clouds. I found myself running without weariness or heaviness of the limbs through the soaked overhanging grass. I knew that I was more than the some-thing which had been looking out all that day upon the visible earth and thinking and speaking and tasting friend-ship. Somewhere – close at hand in that rosy thicket or far off beyond the ribs of sunset – I was gathered up with an immortal company, where I and poet and lover and flower and cloud and star were equals, as all the little leaves were equal ruffling before the gusts, or sleeping and carved out of the silentness. And in that company I had learned that I am something which no fortune can touch, whether I be soon to die or long years away. Things will happen which will trample and pierce, but I shall go on, something that is here and there like the wind, something unconquerable, something not to be separated from the dark earth and the light sky, a strong citizen of infinity and eternity. The confidence and ease had become a deep joy; I knew that I could not do without the Infinite, nor the Infinite without me. (Extract from 'The Stile', *Light and Twilight*, 1911, 46–51)

Practicalities – A Ride in a Cart

'Five o'clock, sir', said the Cockney at my door next morning, and I looked out to see a hot day slowly and certainly preparing in mist and silence. There was nobody in the fields. The hay-waggon stood by the rick where it had arrived too late to be unloaded last night. To one bred in a town this kind of silence and solitariness perhaps always remains impressive. We see no man, no smoke, and hear no voice of man or beast or machinery, and straightway the mind recalls very early mornings when London has lain silent but for the cooing of pigeons. That silence of so many things that can and will make sounds gives some of its prestige to the country silence of very quiet things. Therefore when I have looked out of a strange window for the first time and seen nothing move but leaves on the earth and clouds in the sky, I have often for a moment felt as if it were dawn and have slipped into a mood of dawn; it might be possible on a cloudy day and in a new country to be deceived thus even at noon. Thus the innocence of silent London is transferred to the downs, the woods, the vacant fields, and the road without a wheel or a foot upon it for miles and miles.

I had about forty miles to cover before the end of the daylight, so I had to help myself by driving with my host and his 'old son' John. I was now thoroughly foot-sore. One foot was particularly bad, and in trying to save it I used different muscles in the leg, which were quickly tired. Then, to help myself, I had leaned heavily on my stick at every step and so brought arm and shoulder to a state of discomfort, if not pain. Finally, the stick was unsuitable for its purpose and sorely afflicted the palm of the hand that grasped it. I had carried the stick for many single days of walking and liked it. For it was a tapered oak sapling cut in the Weald and virtually straight because its slightly spiral curves counteracted one another. But it had almost no handle, and so drove itself into one small portion of the palm when leaned on. It had also in the winter shown itself hard to retain in the hand when a few inches of it were in mud. Nevertheless, it was so nicely balanced and being oak so likely to last a lifetime that, for six years, I put up with its faults, and now, having been in my company for so many miles in a splendid June, it has a fresh hold upon me. Also I am not certain that any other handle, a larger and rounder knob or a stout natural crook, would have been much better in a hand not made of iron. Perhaps a really long staff grasped some way from its upper end would be right. But there is something too majestic, patriarchal even, about such a staff. A man would have to build up his life round about it if it had been deliberately adopted. And gradually he would become a celebrity. Of course, if he had an inclination towards such a staff, as the natural and accredited form among pedestrians, there would be an end of the matter, but that is not very likely in a town-bred Englishman. He must meditate upon what might have been, and be content to make five shillings out of his meditation, if he is a journalist.

It was a pleasure to drive with Mr. Willcocks. He became quite silent apart from civility. He evidently understood the horse, and the horse him, in the mutual manner usually expected from a legal monogamous union. If he had sat on the horse's back the combination would have been nothing like a centaur. But with one between the shafts and the other holding the reins they were one spirit in two bodies. (*The Icknield Way*, 145–47)

Walking with Good Company

And in our own muscles and hearts the evening strives to form an aspiration that shall suit the joy of the hills, the meadows, the copses and their people. We will go on, they say; we will go on and on, through the beeches on the hill and up over the ridge and down again through the grey wet meadows and to the old road between hawthorn and guelder-rose at the foot of the downs; and still on, not as before, but out of time and space, until we come – home – to some refuge of beauty and serenity in the heart of the immense evening. And so we will, though we shall be wise to find our achievement in the rapture of walking, or in the short rest upon a gate where we may surprise the twilight at her consecrating task. It is well, too, to talk, not to walk silently and weave such dreams as will make our host to-night intolerable; or if not to talk, then to sing some old song whose melody finds a strange fitness to our minds, in spite of the words [...] (extract from 'Walking with Good Company', Chapter iv, *The Heart of England*, 30)

NOTES AND REFERENCES

32 A 19th century chalk horse.
33 Unknown source.
34 Also called Alphekka or Alpha Coronae Borealis.

Chapter Six

People

Edward Thomas's childhood was recorded in a series of autobiographical and semi-autobiographical works that he produced shortly before turning to poetry. In these he searched for a form and theme that would allow him to express himself more freely than he had been able to in his countryside books. Abercorran House, the setting of *The Happy-go-Lucky Morgans* (1913), is thought to be based on houses, inhabited by Welsh families, that Thomas knew from his childhood in South London. The character of Aurelius, who is described as a visitor to Abercorran House in the third extract, is fictional, possibly used to both deride and analyse some of the characteristics that Thomas saw in himself. This is also the case for the numerous office clerks and 'Other Man' characters in his prose writing, and the poem by that name.

Thomas groups together the itinerant labourers, wounded soldiers, clerks and poets he writes about – he considers them all marginal and easily replaceable in the industrialised economy because they don't produce or consume in sufficient quantities. However, he suggests an alternative system of worth in his writing on Richard Jefferies, William James and Thomas Traherne, where nature and compassion are the true sources of value. The poem 'Aspens' shows how far Thomas understood himself in terms of non-human nature, even going as far as to identify himself with a particular species of tree.

While writing about landscape, Thomas's countryside writing is filled with people and their histories, including other writers who were associated with a particular place (see also his biographies and *A Literary Pilgrim in England*). His writing about his family is concentrated in these autobiographies, and the 'Household Poems'. The poem for his wife, 'And you, Helen', is printed below. Thomas had a notoriously difficult relationship with his father which involved resentment on both sides because his father wanted him to join him in working for the civil service. The extract below shows a happier memory of the Thomas family.

Family – Mother and Father

If I cannot call up images of most of the streets as they were then, because I have witnessed the gradual development since, perhaps the reason is the same for my being unable to call up images of my father and mother or of my brothers. No. I have only one clear early glimpse of my father – darting out of the house in his slippers and chasing and catching a big boy who had bullied me. He was eloquent, confident, black-haired, brown-eyed, all that my mother was not. By glimpses, I learnt with awe and astonishment that he had once been of my age. He knew, for example, far more about marbles than the best players at school. His talk of 'alley-taws' – above all the way his thumb drove the marble out of the crook of his first finger, the speeding sureness of it – these betokened mastery. Once or twice I spent an hour or so in his office in an old government building. The presence of a wash-stand in a sitting-room pleased me, but what pleased me still more was the peculiar large brown caraway biscuit which I never got anywhere else. My father at this time gave or was to have given lessons to Lady Somebody, and he mentioned her to me once when we were together in his office. She became connected somehow with the caraway biscuit. With or without her aid, this rarity had a kind of magic and beauty as of a flower or bird only to be found in one wood in all the world. I can hear but never see him telling me for the tenth or hundredth time the story of the Wiltshire moonrakers hanging in a chain over a bridge to fetch the moon out, which they had mistaken for green cheese, and the topmost one, whose hold on the parapet began slipping, crying out, 'Hold tight below while I spit on my hands,' and many another comic tale or rhyme. My mother I can hardly see save as she is now while I am writing. I cannot see her but I can summon up her presence. She is plainest to me not quite dressed, in white bodice and petticoat, her arms and shoulders rounded and creamy smooth. My affection for her was leavened with lesser likings and with admiration. I liked the scent of her fresh warm skin and supposed it unique. Her straight nose and chin made a profile that for years formed my standard. No hair was so beautiful to me as hers was, light golden brown hair, long and rippling. Her singing at fall of night, especially if we were alone together, soothed and fascin-ated me, as though it had been divine, at once the mightiest and the softest sound in the world. (*The Childhood of Edward Thomas*, 1938, 17–19)

'And you, Helen' (April 1916, *Poems*)

> And you, Helen, what should I give you?
> So many things I would give you
> Had I an infinite great store
> Offered me and I stood before
> To choose. I would give you youth,
> All kinds of loveliness and truth,
> A clear eye as good as mine,
> Lands, waters, flowers, wine,
> As many children as your heart

Might wish for, a far better art
Than mine can be, all you have lost
Upon the travelling waters tossed,
Or given to me. If I could choose
Freely in that great treasure-house
Anything from any shelf,
I would give you back yourself,
And power to discriminate
What you want and want it not too late,
Many fair days free from care
And heart to enjoy both foul and fair,
And myself, too, if I could find
Where it lay hidden and it proved kind.

Vagrants, Labourers, Soldiers and Poets – 'Aurelius, the Superfluous Man'

We recalled many memories, Ann and I, as we stood in the empty and silent, but still sunlit yard, on my last visit. At one moment the past seemed everything, the present a dream; at another, the past seemed to have gone for ever. Trying, I suppose, to make myself believe that there had been no break, but only a gradual change, I asked Ann if things at Abercorran House had not been quieter for some time past.

'Oh no,' said she, 'there was always someone new dropping in, and you know nobody came twice without coming a hundred times. We had the little Morgans of Clare's Castle here for more than a year, and almost crowded us out with friends. Then Mr – whatever was his name – the Italian – I mean the Gypsy – Mr Aurelius – stayed here three times for months on end, and that brought quite little children.'

'Of course it did, Ann. Aurelius … Don't I remember what he was can it be fifteen years ago? He was the first man I ever met who really proved that man is above the other animals *as an animal.* He was really better than any pony, or hound, or bird of prey, in their own way.'

'Now you are *talking*, Mr Froxfield – Arthur, I *should* say.'

'I suppose I am, but Aurelius makes you talk. I remember him up in the Library reading that Arabian tale about the great king who had a hundred thousand kings under him, and what he liked most was to read in old books about Paradise and its wonders and loveliness. I remember Aurelius saying: And when he came upon a certain description of Paradise, its pavilions and lofty chambers and precious-laden trees, and a thousand beautiful and strange things, he fell into a rapture so that he determined to make its equal on earth.'

'He is the first rich man I ever heard of that had so much sense,' said Ann. 'Perhaps Aurelius would have done like that if he had been as rich as sin, instead of owing a wine-and-spirit merchant four and six and being owed half-a-crown by me. But he does not need it now, that is, so far as we can tell.'

'What, Ann, is Aurelius dead?'

'That I cannot say. But we shall never see him again.'

'Why frighten me for nothing? Of course he will turn up: he always did.'

'That is impossible.'

'Why?'

'He promised Mr Torrance he would write and wait for an answer every Midsummer day, if not oftener, wherever he might be. He has now missed two Midsummers, which he would not do – you know he could not do such a thing to Mr Torrance – if he was in his right mind. He wasn't young, and perhaps he had to pay for keeping his young looks so long.'

'Why? How old could he be?' I said quickly, forgetting how long ago it was that I met him first.

'I know he is fifty,' said Ann.

I did not answer because it seemed ridiculous and I did not want to be rude to Ann. I should have said a moment before, had I been asked, that he was thirty. But Ann was right.

'Where was he last heard of, Ann?'

'I went myself with little Henry Morgan and Jessie to a place called Oatham, or something like it, where he last wrote from. He had been an under-gardener there for nearly two years, and we saw the man and his wife who let him a room and looked after him. They said he seemed to be well-off, and of course he would. You know he ate little, smoked and drank nothing, and gave nothing to any known charities. They remembered him very well because he taught them to play cards and was very clean and very silent. "As clean as a lady," she said to Jessie, who only said, "Cleaner". You know her way. The man did not like him, I know. He said Aurelius used to sit as quiet as a book and never complained of anything. "He never ate half he paid for, I will say that," said he. "He was too fond of flowers, too, for an under-gardener, and used to ask why daisies and fluellen and such-like were called weeds. There was something wrong with him, something on his conscience perhaps." The squire's agent, a Mr Theobald, said the same when he came in. He thought there was something wrong. He said such people were unnecessary. Nothing could be done with them. They were no better than wild birds compared with pheasants, even when they could sing, which some of them could do, but not Aurelius. They caused a great deal of trouble, said my lord the agent of my lord the squire, yet you couldn't put them out of the way. He remarked that Aurelius never wrote any letters and never received any – that looked bad, too. "What we want," said he – "is a little less Theobald," said Jessie, but the man didn't notice her. "What we want is efficiency. How are we to get it with the likes of this Mr What's-his-name in the way? They neither produce like the poor nor consume like the rich, and it is by production and consumption that the world goes round, I say. He was a bit of a poacher, too. I caught him myself letting a hare out of a snare – letting it out, so he said. I said nothing to the squire, but the chap had to go." 'And that's all we shall hear about Aurelius,' said Ann. 'He left there in the muck of February. They didn't know where he was going, and didn't care, though he provided them with gossip for a year to come. The woman asked me how old he was. Before I could have answered, her husband said: "About thirty I should say." The woman could not resist saying snappily: "Fifty" …'

Aurelius was gone, then. It cannot have surprised anyone. What was surprising was the way he used to reappear after long absences. While he was present everyone liked him, but he had something unreal about him or not like a man of this world. When that squire's agent called his under-gardener a superfluous man, he was a brute and he was wrong, but he saw straight. If we accept his label there must always have been some superfluous men since the beginning, men whom the extravagant ingenuity of creation has produced out of sheer delight in variety, by-products of its immense processes. Sometimes I think it was some of these superfluous men who invented God and all the gods and godlets. Some of them have been killed, some enthroned, some sainted, for it. But in a civilisation like ours the superfluous abound and even flourish. They are born in palace and cottage and under hedges. Often they are fortunate in being called mad from early years; sometimes they live a brief, charmed life without toil, envied almost as much as the animals by drudges; sometimes they are no more than delicate instruments on which men play melodies of agony and sweetness. (*The Happy-Go-Lucky Morgans*, 1913, 44–62)

The Unemployed

The multitude on the pavement continued to press straight onward, or to flit in and out of coloured shops. None looked at the standard, the dark man and his cloudy followers, except a few of the smallest newspaper boys who had a few spare minutes and rushed over to march with them in the hope of music or a speech or a conflict. The straight flower-girl flashed her eyes as she stood on the kerb, her left arm curving with divine grace round the shawl-hidden child at her bosom, her left hand thrust out full of roses. The tender, well-dressed women leaning on the arms of their men smiled faintly, a little pitiful, but gladly conscious of their own security and pleasantness. Men with the historic sense glanced and noted the fact that there was a procession. One man, standing on the kerb, took a sovereign from his pocket, looked at it and then at the unemployed, made a little gesture of utter bewilderment, and dropping the coin down into the drain below, continued to watch. Comfortable clerks and others of the servile realized that here were the unemployed about whom the newspapers had said this and that – ('a pressing question' – 'a very complicated question not to be decided in a hurry' – 'it is receiving the attention of some of the best intellects of the time' – 'our special reporter is making a full investigation' – 'who are the genuine and who are the impostors?' – 'connected with Socialist intrigues') – and they repeated the word 'Socialism' and smiled at the bare legs of the son of man and the yellow boots of the orator. Next day they would smile again with pride that they had seen the procession which ended in feeble, violent speeches against the Army and the Rich, in four arrests and an imprisonment. For they were angry and uttered curses. One waved an arm against a palace, an arm that could scarcely hold out a revolver even were all the kings sitting in a row to tempt him. In the crowd and disturbance the leader fell and fainted. They propped him in their arms and cleared a space about him. 'Death of Nelson,' suggested an onlooker, laughing, as he observed the attitude and the knee-breeches. 'If he had only a crown of thorns ... ' said another, pleased by the group. 'Wants a bit of skilly and real hard work,' said a third. (*The South Country*, 93–4)

'Man and Dog' (January 1915, *Last Poems*)

> ''Twill take some getting.' 'Sir, I think 'twill so.'
> The old man stared up at the mistletoe
> That hung too high in the poplar's crest for
>   plunder
> Of any climber, though not for kissing under:
> Then he went on against the north-east wind –
> Straight but lame, leaning on a staff new-skinned,
> Carrying a brolly, flag-basket, and old coat, –
> Towards Alton, ten miles off. And he had not
> Done less from Chilgrove where he pulled up docks.
> 'Twere best, if he had had 'a money-box,'

To have waited there till the sheep cleared a field
For what a half-week's flint-picking would yield.
His mind was running on the work he had done
Since he left Christchurch in the New Forest, one
Spring in the 'seventies, — navvying on dock and
  line
From Southampton to Newcastle-on-Tyne, —
In 'seventy-four a year of soldiering
With the Berkshires, — hoeing and harvesting
In half the shires where corn and couch will
  grow.
His sons, three sons, were fighting, but the hoe
And reap-hook he liked, or anything to do with
  trees.
He fell once from a poplar tall as these:
The Flying Man they called him in hospital.
'If I flew now, to another world I'd fall.'
He laughed and whistled to the small brown
  bitch
With spots of blue that hunted in the ditch.
Her foxy Welsh grandfather must have paired
Beneath him. He kept sheep in Wales and scared
Strangers, I will warrant, with his pearl eye
And trick of shrinking off as he were shy,
Then following close in silence for — for what?
'No rabbit, never fear, she ever got,
Yet always hunts. Today she nearly had one:
She would and she wouldn't. 'Twas like that.
    The bad one!
She's not much use, but still she's company,
Though I'm not. She goes everywhere with me.
So Alton I must reach to-night somehow:
I'll get no shakedown with that bedfellow

From farmers. Many a man sleeps worse to-night
Than I shall.' 'In the trenches.' 'Yes, that's right.
But they'll be out of that – I hope they be –
This weather, marching after the enemy.'
'And so I hope. Good luck.' And there I nodded
'Good-night. You keep straight on.' Stiffly he
    plodded;
And at his heels the crisp leaves scurried fast,
And the leaf-coloured robin watched.
    They passed,
The robin till next day, the man for good,
Together in the twilight of the wood.

'Hampshire – An Umbrella Man' (extract)

A perambulator with a cabbage in it stood at one corner; leaning against it was an ebony-handled umbrella and two or three umbrella- frames; underneath it an old postman's bag containing a hammer and other tools. Close by stood half a loaf on a newspaper, several bottles of bright water, a black pot of potatoes ready for boiling, a tin of water steaming against a small fire of hazel twigs. Out on the sunny grass two shirts were drying. In the midst was the proprietor, his name revealed in fresh chalk on the side of his perambulator: 'John Clark, Hampshire'.

He had spent his last pence on potatoes and had been given the cabbage. No one would give him work on a Sunday. He had no home, no relations. Being deaf, he did not look for company. So he stood up, to get dry and to think, think, think, his hands on his hips, while he puffed at an empty pipe. During his meditation a snail had crawled half-way up his trousers, and was now all but down again. He was of middle height and build, the crookedest of men, yet upright, like a branch of oak which comes straight with all its twistings. His head was small and round, almost covered by bristly grey hair like lichen, through which peered quiet blue eyes; the face was irregular, almost shapeless, like dough being kneaded, worn by travel, passion, pain, and not a few blows; where the skin was visible at all through the hair it was like red sandstone; his teeth were white and strong and short like an old dog's. His rough neck descended into a striped half-open shirt, to which was added a loose black waistcoat divided into thin perpendicular stripes by ribs of faded gold; his trousers, loose and patched and short, approached the colour of a hen pheasant; his bare feet were partly hidden by old black boots. His voice was hoarse and, for one of his enduring look, surprisingly small, and produced with an effort and a slight jerk of the head.

He was a Sussex man, born in the year 1831, on June the twenty-first (it seemed a foppery in him to remember the day, and it was impossible to imagine with what ceremony he had remembered it year by year, during half a century or near it, on the roads of Sussex, Kent, Surrey and Hampshire). His mother was a Wild – there were several of them buried not far away under the carved double-headed tombstones by the old church with the lancet windows and the four yews. He was a labourer's son, and he had already had a long life of hoeing and reaping and fagging when he enlisted at Chatham. He had kept his musket bright, slept hard and wet, and starved on thirteenpence a day, moving from camp to camp every two years. He had lost his youth in battle, for a bullet went through his knee; he lay four months in hospital, and they took eighteen pieces of bone out of his wound – he was still indignant because he was described as only 'slightly wounded' when he was discharged after a 'short service' of thirteen years. He showed his gnarled knee to explain his crookedness. Little he could tell of the battle except the sobbing of the soldier next to him – 'a London chap from Haggerston way. Lord! he called for his mother and his God and me to save him, and the noise he made was worse than the firing and the groaning of the horses, and I was just thinking how I could stop his mouth for him when a bullet hits me, and down I goes like a baby.'

He had been on the road forty years. For a short time after his discharge he worked on the land and lived in a cottage with his wife and one child. The church bells were beginning to ring, and I asked him if he was going to church. At first he said nothing, but looked down at his striped waistcoat and patched trousers; then, with a quick violent gesture of scorn, he lifted up his head and even threw it back before he spoke. 'Besides,' he said, 'I remember how it was my little girl died – My little girl, says I, but she would have been a big handsome woman now, forty-eight years old on the first of May that is gone. She was lying in bed with a little bit of a cough, and she was gone as white as a lily, and I went in to her when I came home from reaping. I saw she looked bad and quiet-like – like a fish in a hedge – and something came over me, and I caught hold of both her hands in both of mine and held them tight, and put my head close up to hers and said, 'Now look here, Polly, you've got to get well. Your mother and me can't stand losing you. And you aren't meant to die; such a one as you be for a lark.' And I squeezed her little hands, and all my nature seemed to rise up and try to make her get well. Polly she looked whiter than ever and afraid; I suppose I was a bit rough and dirty and sunburnt, for 'twas a hot harvest and 'twas the end of the second week of it, and I was that fierce I felt I ought to have had my way … All that night I thought I had done a wrong thing trying to keep her from dying that way, and I tell you I cried in case I had done any harm by it … That very night she died without our knowing it. She was a bonny maid, that fond of flowers. The night she was taken ill she was coming home with me from the Thirteen Acre, where I'd been hoeing the mangolds, and she had picked a rose for her mother. All of a sudden she looks at it and says, "It's gone, it's broke, it's gone, it's gone, gone, gone," and she kept on, "It's broke, it's gone, it's gone," and when she got home she ran up to her mother, crying, "The wild rose is broke, mother; broke, gone, gone," she says, just like that,' said the old man, in a high finical voice more like that of a bird than a child …

'Then my old woman – well, she was only a bit of a wench too; seventeen when we were married – she took ill and died within a week after … There was a purpose in it … It was then the end of harvest. I spent all my wages down at the Fighting Cocks, and then I set out to walk to Mildenhall in Wiltshire, where my wife came from. On the way I met a chap I had quarrelled with in Egypt, and he says to me, ' Hullo, Scrammy-handed Jack,' with a sort of look, and I, not thinking what I did, I set about him, and before I knew it he was lying there as might be dead, and I went and gave myself up, and I don't mind saying that I wished I might be hanged for it. However, I did six months. That was how I came to be in the umbrella line. I took up with a chap who did a bit of tinkering and umbrella-mending and grinding in the roving way, and a job of hoeing or mowing now and then. He died not so very long after in the year of the siege of Paris, and I have been alone ever since. Nor I haven't been to church since, any more than a blackbird would go and perch on the shoulder of one of those ladies with feathers and wings and a bit of a fox in their hats.'

Labourer, soldier, labourer, tinker, umbrella man, he had always wandered, and knew the South Country between Fordingbridge and Dover as a man knows his garden. Every village, almost every farmhouse, especially if there were hops on the land, he knew, and could see with his blue eyes as he remembered them and spoke their names. I never met a man who knew England as he did. (*The South Country*, 188–92)

'As the team's head-brass' (May 1916, *Poems*)

> As the team's head-brass flashed out on the turn
> The lovers disappeared into the wood.
> I sat among the boughs of the fallen elm
> That strewed an angle of the fallow, and
> Watched the plough narrowing a yellow square
> Of charlock. Every time the horses turned
> Instead of treading me down, the ploughman
>   leaned
> Upon the handles to say or ask a word,
> About the weather, next about the war.
> Scraping the share he faced towards the wood,
> And screwed along the furrow till the brass flashed
> Once more.
>   The blizzard felled the elm whose crest
> I sat in, by a woodpecker's round hole,
> The ploughman said. 'When will they take it
>   away?'
> 'When the war's over.' So the talk began –

One minute and an interval of ten,
A minute more and the same interval.
Have you been out ?' 'No.' 'And don't want to,
    perhaps?'
'If I could only come back again, I should.
I could spare an arm. I shouldn't want to lose
A leg. If I should lose my head, why, so,
I should want nothing more ... Have many gone
From here ?' 'Yes.' 'Many lost?' 'Yes: a good few.
Only two teams work on the farm this year.
One of my mates is dead. The second day
In France they killed him. It was back in March,
The very night of the blizzard, too. Now if
He had stayed here we should have moved
    the tree.'
'And I should not have sat here. Everything
Would have been different. For it would have
    been
Another world.' 'Ay, and a better, though
If we could see all all might seem good.' Then
The lovers came out of the wood again:
The horses started and for the last time
I watched the clods crumble and topple over
After the ploughshare and the stumbling team.

Writers – Thomas Traherne

No English writer has expressed as well as Traherne the spiritual glory of childhood, in which Wordsworth saw intimations of immortality. He speaks of 'that divine light wherewith I was born' and of his 'pure and virgin apprehensions,' and recommends his friend to pray earnestly for these gifts: 'They will make you angelical, and wholly celestial'. It was by the 'divine knowledge' that he saw all things in the peace of Eden –

> The corn was orient and immortal wheat, which never should be reaped, nor was ever sown. I thought it had stood from everlasting to everlasting. The dust and stones of the street were as precious as gold; the gates were at first the end of the world. The green trees when I saw them first through one of the gates transported and ravished me; their sweetness and unusual beauty made my heart to leap and almost mad with ecstasy; they were such strange and wonderful things. The Men! O what venerable and reverend creatures did the aged seem! Immortal Cherubims! And young men glittering and sparkling angels, and maids strange seraphic pieces of life and beauty! Boys and girls tumbling in the street, and playing, were moving jewels. I knew not that they were born or should die; but all things abided eternally as they were in their proper places. Eternity was manifest in the light of the day, and something infinite behind everything appeared, which tallied with my expectation and moved my desire …
> – Thomas Traherne, *Centuries of Meditations,* edited by Bertram Dobell (London: Dobell, 1908) 157.

Yet was this light eclipsed. He was 'with much ado' perverted by the world, by the temptation of men and worldly things and by 'opinion and custom,' not any 'inward corruption or depravation of Nature'.

For he tells us how he once entered a noble dining-room and was there alone 'to see the gold and state and carved imagery,' but wearied of it because it was dead, and had no motion. A little afterwards he saw it 'full of lords and ladies and music and dancing,' and now pleasure took the place of tediousness, and he perceived, long after, that 'men and women are, when well understood, a principal part of our true felicity' [174]. Once again, 'in a lowering and sad evening, being alone in the field, when all things were dead quiet,' he had the same weariness, nay, even horror. 'I was a weak and little child, and had forgotten there was a man alive in the earth.' Nevertheless, hope and expectation came to him and comforted him, and taught him 'that he was concerned in all the world.' That he was 'concerned in all the world' was the great source of comfort and joy which he found in life, and of that joy which his book pours out for us. Not only did he see that he was concerned in all the world, but that river and corn and herb and sand were so concerned. God, he says, 'knoweth infinite excellencies' in each of these things; 'He seeth how it relateth to angels and men'. In this he anticipated Blake's *Auguries of Innocence*. He seems to see the patterns which all living things are for ever weaving. He would have men strive after this divine knowledge of things and of their place in the universe. (*The South Country*, 131–33)

Richard Jefferies

In 'Sunlight in a London Square' [from Richard Jefferies' 1884 collection *The Life of the Fields*] the thought of the reapers sadly labouring sends him forward to 'a race able to enjoy the flowers with which the physical work is strewn'. For himself and others he desires longer, more joyous life, and the passion of his wish seems half a realization; he desires it for the very birds – 'a hundred years just to feast on the seeds and sing and be utterly happy and oblivious of everything but the moment they are passing'. In the same mood comes a pleading for wiser treatment of 'the sullen poor who stand scornful and desperate at the street-corners'. The holy spring, the water and the light, give him of their truth, of the sense of beauty which they bring with them; in his love of its purity there is an even profounder sentiment than in Ruskin's passionate upbraiding of those who defiled the Wandel springs. In 'The Pageant of Summer' the hope is repeated: 'Earth holds secrets enough to give them the life of the fabled Immortals'. Part at least of the charm of that and the kindred essays lies in the linking of spiritual things to their physical causes among the coombes, the long wavering heights, the barley and the grass, of the Downs, and the flowers of Coate Farm itself. Earth, the mighty mother, emerges almost personified in these essays, benign, abundant, hale. In 'Beauty in the Country' he says that it takes a hundred and fifty years to make a beauty – a hundred and fifty years out of doors ... All beautiful women come from the country'.

The Wind and the Wheat speak these same things in 'St. Guido' [from *The Open Air*, 1885], Joy in Nature 'makes today a thousand years long backwards and a thousand years long forwards'. The Wheat is glad to be cut down for men's sakes, knowing its tribe cannot die, 'but there is one thing we do not like, and that is all the labour and the misery which ends in nothing, not even a flower'. The Wheat goes on:

'All the thousand years of labour since this field was first ploughed have not stored up anything for you. It would not matter about the work so much if you were only happy; the bees work every year, but they are happy; the doves build a nest every year, but they are very, very happy. We think it must be because you do not come out to us and be with us, and think more as we do. It is not because your people have not got plenty to eat and drink – you have as much as the bees. Why, just look at us! Look at the wheat that grows all over the world; all the figures that were ever written in pencil could not tell how much, it is such an immense quantity. Yet your people starve and die of hunger every now and then, and we have seen the wretched beggars tramping along the road. We have known of times when there was a great pile of us, almost a hill piled up; it was not in this country, it was in another warmer country, and yet no one dared to touch it – they died at the bottom of the hill of wheat. The earth is full of skeletons of people who have died of hunger. They are dying now this minute in your big cities, with nothing but stones all round them – stone walls and stone streets; not jolly stones like those you threw in the water, dear – hard, unkind stones that make them cold and let them die, while we are growing here, millions of us, in the sunshine with the butterflies floating over us. This makes us unhappy; I was very unhappy this morning till you came running over and played with us.'

'It is not because there is not enough: it is because your people are so short-sighted, so jealous and selfish, and so curiously infatuated with things that are not so good as your old toys which you have flung away and forgotten. And you teach the children hum, hum, all day to care about such silly things, and to work for them and to look to them as the object of their lives. It is because you do not share us among you without price or difference; because you do not share the great earth among you fairly, without spite and jealousy and avarice; because you will not agree; you silly, foolish people to let all the flowers wither for a thousand years while you keep each other at a distance, instead of agreeing and sharing them! Is there something in you – as there is poison in the nightshade, you know it, dear, your papa told you not to touch it – is there a sort of poison in your people that works them up into a hatred of one another? Why, then, do you not agree and have all things, all the great earth can give you, just as we have the sunshine and the rain? How happy your people could be if they would only agree! But you go on teaching even the little children to follow the same silly objects, hum, hum, hum, all the day, and they will grow up to hate each other, and to try which can get the most round things – you have one in your pocket.'

'Sixpence,' said Guido. 'It's quite a new one.'

It is naughty Socialistic Wheat. Then, again, in 'One of the New Voters,' Roger the reaper has swallowed a gallon of harvest beer, 'probably the vilest drink in the world': 'upon this abominable mess the golden harvest of English fields is gathered in'. Next day he can eat no breakfast, but he drinks more of the beer, and works fourteen hours, then to the inn. 'I think,' says Jefferies, 'it would need a very clever man indeed to invent something for him to do, some way for him to spend his evening'. He sees no way out; no way of blunting the contrast between the golden sun and wheat and the harvest slave. He has come to see that the labourer's life is not, as the *Times* said in 1872, 'that life of competency without care which poets dream of'; he has even found that harvest wages may be earned too hard. He sees no way out. He states an evil, and dimly sees a good. He has discovered something divine in Nature with which he cannot reconcile men as they are. But he takes refuge in no fortress of dreams; he never forgets, he would never desert, men and the present. 'The forest is gone,' he writes at Eltham, ' but the spirit of Nature stays, and can be found by those who search for it. Dearly as I love the open air, I cannot regret the medieval days. I do not wish them back again; I would sooner fight in the foremost ranks of Time. Nor do we need them, for the spirit of Nature stays, and will always be here, no matter to how high a pinnacle of thought the human mind may attain; still the sweet air, and the hills, and the sea, and the sun, will always be with us.'

But these essays are not to be judged by the thoughts which occur in them. In the best he has created poetry that gushes naturally, thought, emotion, and sensuous picture, out of the loving contemplation of visible things.

There are at least four ways of looking at visible things. Take, for example, a rough, thistly meadow at night.

One man sees a multitude of tall, pale thistles in a field of grey moonlight, knows them to be thistles, acknowledges the fact, and passes on without pause.

One is startled by their appearance. They are unlike thistles or any other plants as seen by day, and he has never seen them so before. He stops to make sure what they are, and at last remembers seeing them in a commonplace light by day, and he allows the first impression to die away.

Another sees them, and is startled, utterly forgetful that there was anything there when he passed before. He cannot reason about them, is too lazy or excited to go over and touch and see; he returns home with a tale of the unusual moonlight growth in the field at the edge of the wood. In an earlier age he might have reported the seeing of a mushroom flourishing of fairies.

Another sees them with a rapt placidity as something beautiful and new, and his recollection or discovery that they are thistles does not disturb his enjoyment. His eye and heart feed together upon their strangeness and beauty. He has really captured one of the visions which clear eyes and an untarnished soul are summoning continually from inexhaustible and eternal Nature.

Jefferies is often like the first, and the result of this kind of vision is his most pedestrian essay; at his best, as in 'The Pageant of Summer,' he is like the last. Being a prose-writer, he cannot change the things themselves – flower, and leaf, and sky – into melody and words, as the poet can in verse. Prose is by its nature discursive and explanatory, and Jefferies brings the objects before the eyes, and gradually, by means of a phrase, a comment, or a thought arising out of them, invests them with the spirit of life which gave them their first significance to him. Description and meditation, a beating heart and memory aiding, grow and intertwine with all the apparently ungoverned life of copse or meadow that comes to have a separate identity of its own. He seeks no neatness or balance, is impatient of the devices of the city-bred artist. 'Is all the world,' he asks, 'to be Versaillised?' (*Richard Jefferies: His Life and Work*, 1909, 213–17)

The Other Man – 'Aspens' (July 1915, *Last Poems*)

> All day and night, save winter, every weather,
> Above the inn, the smithy, and the shop,
> The aspens at the cross-roads talk together
> Of rain, until their last leaves fall from the top.
>
> Out of the blacksmith's cavern comes the ringing
> Of hammer, shoe, and anvil; out of the inn
> The clink, the hum, the roar, the random singing –
> The sounds that for these fifty years have been.

The whisper of the aspens is not drowned,
And over lightless pane and footless road,
Empty as sky, with every other sound
Not ceasing, calls their ghosts from their abode,

A silent smithy, a silent inn, nor fails
In the bare moonlight or the thick-furred gloom,
In tempest or the night of nightingales,
To turn the cross-roads to a ghostly room.

And it would be the same were no house near.
Over all sorts of weather, men, and times,
Aspens must shake their leaves and men may hear
But need not listen, more than to my rhymes.

Whatever wind blows while they and I have leaves
We cannot other than an aspen be
That ceaselessly, unreasonably grieves,
Or so men think who like a different tree.

The Reappearance of the Other Man

At that point a man entered whom I slowly recognized as
the liberator of the chaffinch on Good Friday. At first I
did not grasp the connection between this dripping,
indubitably real man and the wraith of the day before.
But he was absurdly pleased to recognize me, bowing
with a sort of uncomfortable graciousness and a trace of a
cockney accent. His expression changed in those few
moments from a melancholy and too yielding smile to a
pale, thin-lipped rigidity. I did not know whether to be
pleased or not with the reincarnation, when he departed to
change his clothes.

This Other Man, as I shall call him, ate his supper in

silence, and then adjusted himself in the armchair, stretching himself out so that all of him was horizontal except his head. He was smoking a cigarette dejectedly, for he had left his pipe behind at Romsey. I offered him a clay pipe. No; he would not have it. They stuck to his lips, he said. But he volunteered to talk about clay pipes, and the declining industry of manufacturing them. (From 'Guildford to Durbridge', *In Pursuit of Spring*, 119–20)

[second extract]

'I suppose you write books,' said I. 'I do,' said he. 'What sort of books do you write?' 'I wrote one all about this valley of the Frome … But no one knows that it was the Frome I meant. You look surprised. Nevertheless, I got fifty pounds for it'. 'That is a lot of money for such a book!' 'So my publisher thought'.'And you are lucky to get money for doing what you like.' 'What I like!' he muttered, pushing his bicycle back uphill, past the goats by the ruin, and up the steps between walls that were lovely with humid moneywort, and saxifrage like filigree, and ivy-leaved toadflax. Apparently the effort loosened his tongue. He rambled on and on about himself, his past, his writing, his digestion; his main point being that he did not like writing. He had been attempting the impossible task of reducing undigested notes about all sorts of details to a grammatical, continuous narrative. He abused note-books violently. He said that they blinded him to nearly everything that would not go into the form of notes; or, at any rate, he could never afterwards reproduce the great effects of Nature and fill in the interstices merely – which was all they were good for – from the notes. The notes – often of things which he would otherwise have forgotten – had to fill the whole canvas.

Whereas, if he had taken none, then only the important, what he truly cared for, would have survived in his memory, arranged not perhaps as they were in Nature, but at least according to the tendencies of his own spirit. 'Good God!' said he. But luckily we were by this time on the level. I mounted. He followed. (from 'Trowbridge to Shepton Mallet', *In Pursuit of Spring*, 219–20)

'The Other' (December 1914, *Last Poems*)

> The forest ended. Glad I was
> To feel the light, and hear the hum
> Of bees, and smell the drying grass
> And the sweet mint, because I had come
> To an end of forest, and because
> Here was both road and inn, the sum
> Of what's not forest. But 'twas here
> They asked me if I did not pass
> Yesterday this way? 'Not you? Queer.'
> 'Who then? and slept here?' I felt fear.
>
> I learnt his road and, ere they were
> Sure I was I, left the dark wood
> Behind, kestrel and woodpecker,
> The inn in the sun, the happy mood
> When first I tasted sunlight there.
> I travelled fast, in hopes I should
> Outrun that other. What to do
> When caught, I planned not. I pursued
> To prove the likeness, and, if true,
> To watch until myself I knew.
>
> I tried the inns that evening
> Of a long gabled high-street grey,

Of courts and outskirts, travelling
An eager but a weary way,
In vain. He was not there. Nothing
Told me that ever till that day
Had one like me entered those doors,
Save once. That time I dared: 'You may
Recall' – but never-foamless shores
Make better friends than those dull boors.

Many and many a day like this
Aimed at the unseen moving goal
And nothing found but remedies
For all desire. These made not whole;
They sowed a new desire, to kiss
Desire's self beyond control,
Desire of desire. And yet
Life stayed on within my soul.
One night in sheltering from the wet
I quite forgot I could forget.

A customer, then the landlady
Stared at me. With a kind of smile
They hesitated awkwardly:
Their silence gave me time for guile.
Had anyone called there like me,
I asked. It was quite plain the wile
Succeeded. For they poured out all.
And that was naught. Less than a mile
Beyond the inn, I could recall
He was like me in general.

He had pleased them, but I less.
I was more eager than before
To find him out and to confess,
To bore him and to let him bore.

I could not wait: children might guess
I had a purpose, something more
That made an answer indiscreet.
One girl's caution made me sore,
Too indignant even to greet
That other had we chanced to meet.

I sought then in solitude.
The wind had fallen with the night; as still
The roads lay as the ploughland rude,
Dark and naked, on the hill.
Had there been ever any feud
'Twixt earth and sky, a mighty will
Closed it: the crocketed dark trees,
A dark house, dark impossible
Cloud-towers, one star, one lamp, one peace
Held on an everlasting lease:

And all was earth's, or all was sky's;
No difference endured between
The two. A dog barked on a hidden rise;
A marshbird whistled high unseen;
The latest waking blackbird's cries
Perished upon the silence keen.
The last light filled a narrow firth
Among the clouds. I stood serene,
And with a solemn quiet mirth,
An old inhabitant of earth.

Once the name I gave to hours
Like this was melancholy, when
It was not happiness and powers
Coming like exiles home again,
And weaknesses quitting their bowers,
Smiled and enjoyed, far off from men,

Moments of everlastingness.
And fortunate my search was then
While what I sought, nevertheless,
That I was seeking, I did not guess.

That time was brief: once more at inn
And upon road I sought my man
Till once amid a tap-room's din
Loudly he asked for me, began
To speak, as if it had been a sin,
Of how I thought and dreamed and ran
After him thus, day after day:
He lived as one under a ban
For this: what had I got to say?
I said nothing, I slipped away.

And now I dare not follow after
Too close. I try to keep in sight,
Dreading his frown and worse his laughter.
I steal out of the wood to light;
I see the swift shoot from the rafter
By the inn door: ere I alight
I wait and hear the starlings wheeze
And nibble like ducks: I wait his flight.
He goes: I follow: no release
Until he ceases. Then I also shall cease.

Chapter Seven

Buildings and Towns

Although he is known as a countryside writer, Edward Thomas loved aspects of city life, in London, Oxford and in Swansea, particularly in parks and open spaces. He enjoyed what was wild, ancient or evocative; places that embodied the combined work of many different lives, and landscapes that were full of visual or imaginative contrasts. For this reason he did not enjoy new towns or suburbs because of their lack of history which he saw as a kind of illegibility; conversely, he did not like cathedrals, which he thought aimed too much at permanence. Instead, he enjoyed places where man and nature seemed to have come to some sort of mutual tolerance, and which showed respect for the fleetingness of all life.

As a result of his walking adventures, Thomas encountered many types of settlement and dwelling. He was interested in buildings and what they told us about their builders and he wanted to write a book about houses, although it was never commissioned. He did write a book of literary geography called *A Literary Pilgrim in England*, but it was not a work of which he was especially proud, nicknaming it ''Omes and 'Aunts'. From these prose and poetry extracts on place we can see Thomas's development from the disengaged aesthete he refers to in the excerpt from *Oxford*, to the journalist, critic and poet that he became.

Thomas grew up in Lambeth, Battersea and Clapham, attending six different schools. As an undergraduate he spent time in Cowley Road and Lincoln College, Oxford. After he married Helen they first rented rooms in Earlsfield and then in Balham, before moving to Kent in 1901. Edward Thomas lived in many other houses during his adult life: three different houses in Steep, Hampshire, between 1906 and 1916, and two houses in Kent between 1901 and 1906. Additionally, he spent a great deal of time away as a guest or lodger working on his many commissioned books – from East Grinsted to Suffolk, and with Robert Frost in Gloucestershire in 1914. He lived in various army camps with the Artists Rifles and the Royal Garrison Artillery, as described in the poem "'Home'", below, and lived in a house at High Beech, near Loughton, in Essex before finally being stationed at Arras in France.

Accidental Tourism – Small Towns, Churches and Chapels

Most of the towns are small market towns, manufacturing chiefly beer; or they are swollen, especially in the neighbourhood of London, as residential quarters on lines of railway or as health and pleasure resorts on the sea. But any man used to maps will be wiser on these matters in an hour than I am. For what I have sought is quiet and as complete a remoteness as possible from towns, whether of manufactures, of markets or of cathedrals. I have used a good many maps in my time, largely to avoid the towns; but I confess that I prefer to do without them and to go, if I have some days before me, guided by the hills or the sun or a stream – or, if I have one day only, in a rough circle, trusting, by taking a series of turnings to the left or a series to the right, to take much beauty by surprise and to return at last to my starting-point. On a dull day or cloudy night I have often no knowledge of the points of the compass. I never go out to see anything. The signboards thus often astonish me. I wish, by the way, that I had noted down more of the names on the signboards at cross-roads. There is a wealth of poetry in them, as in that which points – by

a ford, too – first, to Poulner and Ringwood; second, to
Gorley and Fordingbridge; third, to Linwood and Broomy;
and another pointing to Fordingbridge, to Ringwood, and
to Cuckoo Hill and Furze Hill: and another in the parish
of Pentlow, pointing to Foxearth and Sudbury, to Caven-
dish and Clare, and to Belchamps and Yeldham. Castles,
churches, old houses, of extraordinary beauty or interest,
have never worn out any of my shoe leather except by
accident. I like to come upon them usually without
knowing their names and legends but do not lament when
chance takes me a hundred times out of their way […] I
prefer any country church or chapel to Winchester or
Chichester or Canterbury Cathedral, just as I prefer 'All
round my hat,' or 'Somer is icumen in,' [British folk songs]
to Beethoven. Not that I dislike the cathedrals, or that I
do not find many pleasures amongst them. But they are
incomprehensible and not restful. I feel when I am within
them that I know why a dog bays at the moon. They are
much more difficult or, rather, I am more conscious in
them of my lack of comprehension, than the hills or the
sea; and I do not like the showmen, the smell and look of
the museum, the feeling that it is admiration or nothing,
and all the well-dressed and fly-blown people round about.
I sometimes think that religious architecture is a dead
language, majestic but dead, that it never was a popular
language. Have some of these buildings lived too long, been
too well preserved, so as to oppress our little days with
too permanent an expression of the passing things? The
truth is that, though the past allures me, and to discover
a cathedral for myself would be an immense pleasure, I
have no historic sense and no curiosity. I mention these
trivial things because they may be important to those who
read what I am paid for writing. I have read a great deal of

history in fact, a university gave me a degree out of respect for my apparent knowledge of history but I have forgotten it all, or it has got into my blood and is present in me in a form which defies evocation or analysis. But as far as I can tell I am pure of history. Consequently I prefer the old brick houses round the cathedral, and that avenue of archaic bossy limes to the cathedral itself with all its turbulent quiet and vague antiquity. (*The South Country*, 3–5)

A Stone Farm

A crossing of roads encloses a waste place of no man's land, of dwarf oaks, hawthorn, bramble and fern, and the flowers of knapweed and harebell, and golden tormentil embroidering the heather and the minute seedling oaks. Follow one of these roads past straight avenues of elms leading up to a farm (built square of stone, under a roof of thatch or stone slate, and lying well back from the road across a level meadow with some willows in the midst, elms round about, willow herb waving rosy by the stream at the border), or merely to a cluster of ricks; and presently the hedges open wide apart and the level white road cools itself under the many trees of a green, wych elms, sycamores, limes and horse-chestnuts, by a pool, and, on the other side, the sign of the 'White Hart,' its horns held back upon its haunches. A stone-built farm and its barns and sheds lie close to the green on either side, and another of more stateliness where the hedges once more run close together alongside the road. This farmhouse has three dormers, two rows of five shadowy windows below, and an ivied porch not quite in the centre; a modest lawn divided by a straight path; dense, well-watered borders of grey lavender, rosemary, ladslove,[35] halberds of crimson

hollyhock, infinite blending stars of Michaelmas daisy; old
apple trees seeming to be pulled down almost to the grass
by glossy-rinded fruit: and, behind, the bended line of hills
a league away, wedding the lowly meadows, the house and
the trees to the large heavens and their white procession of
clouds out of the south and the sea. The utmost kindliness
of earth is expressed in these three houses, the trees on the
flat green, the slightly curving road across it, the uneven
posts and rails leaning this way and that at the edge of the
pond. The trees are so arranged about the road that they
weave a harmony of welcome, of blessing, a viaticum for
whosoever passes by and only for a moment tastes their
shade, acknowledges unconsciously their attitudes, hears
their dry summer murmuring, sees the house behind them.
The wayfarer knows nothing of those who built them and
those who live therein, of those who planted the trees
just so and not otherwise, of the causes that shaped the
green, any more than of those who reaped and threshed the
barley, and picked and dried and packed the hops that
made the ale at the 'White Hart'. (*The South Country* 12–14)

'The Sheiling' (November 1916, *Poems*)

> It stands alone
> Up in a land of stone
> All worn like ancient stairs,
> A land of rocks and trees
> Nourished on wind and stone.
>
> And all within
> Long delicate has been;
> By arts and kindliness
> Coloured, sweetened, and warmed
> For many years has been.

Safe resting there
Men hear in the travelling air
But music, pictures see
In the same daily land
Painted by the wild air.

One maker's mind
Made both, and the house is kind
To the land that gave it peace,
And the stone has taken the house
To its cold heart and is kind.

An Imaginative History

A deeply-worn, narrow and disused track joining it more than half-way down suggests that the lower part was made by the widening of an old road; but much of the upper half is new. Certainly the road as it now is, broad and gently bending round the steep coombe, is new, and it was made at the expense of the last of a family which had long owned the manor house near the entrance of the coombe. His were all the hanging beech woods – huge as the sky – upon the hill, and through them the road-makers conducted this noble and pleasant way. But near the top they deviated by a few yards into another estate. The owner would not give way. A lawsuit was begun, and it was not over when the day came for the road to be open for traffic according to the contract or, if not, to pass out of the defaulter's hands. The day passed; the contract was broken; the speculation had failed, and the tolls would never fill the pockets of the lord of the manor. He was ruined, and left his long white house by the rivulet and its chain of pools, his farms and cottages, his high fruit walls, his uncounted beeches, the home of a hundred owls, his Spanish chestnuts above the rocky lane, his horse-chestnut and sycamore stately in groups, his mighty wych elms, his apple trees and all their mistletoe, his walnut trees, and the long bay of sky that was framed by his tall woods east and north and west.

There are many places which nobody can look upon without being consciously influenced by a sense of their history. It is a battlefield, and the earth shows the scars of its old wounds; or a castle or cathedral of distinct renown rises among the oaks; or a manor house or cottage, or tomb or woodland walk that speaks of a dead poet or soldier. Then, according to the extent or care of our reading and the clearness of our imagination, we can pour into the groves or on the turf tumultuous or silent armies, or solitary man or woman. It is a deeply-worn coast; the spring tide gnaws the yellow cliff, and the wind files it with unceasing hiss, and the relics of every age, skull and weapon and shroud pin and coin and carven stone, are spread out upon the clean, untrodden sand, and the learned, the imaginative, the fanciful, the utterly unhistoric and merely human man exercises his spirit upon them, and responds, if only for a moment. In some places history has wrought like an earthquake, in others like an ant or mole; everywhere, permanently; so that if we but knew or cared, every swelling of the grass, every wavering line of hedge or path or road were an inscription, brief as an epitaph, in many languages and characters. But most of us know only a few of these unspoken languages of the past, and only a few words in each. Wars and parliaments are but dim, soundless, and formless happenings in the brain; toil and passion of generations produce only an enriching of the light within the glades, and a solemnizing of the shadows. (*The South Country*, 149–50)

Cities – London

The wind blew from the northwest with such peace and energy together as to call up the image of a good giant striding along with superb gestures – like those of a sower sowing. The wind blew and the sun shone over London. A myriad roofs laughed together in the light. The smoke and the flags, yellow and blue and white, waved tumultuously, straining for joy to leave the chimneys and the flagstaffs, like hounds sighting their quarry. The ranges of cloud bathing their lower slopes in the brown mist of the horizon had the majesty of great hills, the coolness and sweetness and whiteness of the foam on the crests of the crystal fountains, and they were burning with light. The clouds did honour to the city, which they encircled as with heavenly ramparts. The stone towers and spires were soft, and luminous as old porcelain. There was no substance to be seen that was not made precious by the strong wind and the light divine. All was newly built to a great idea. The flags were waving to salute the festal opening of the gates in those white walls to a people that should presently surge in and onward to take possession. Princely was to be the life that had this amphitheatre of clouds and palaces for its display.

Of human things, only music – if human it can be called – was fit to match this joyousness and this stateliness. What, I thought, if the pomp of river and roof and cloudy mountain walls of the world be made ready, as so often they had been before, only for the joy of the invisible gods? For who has not known a day when some notable festival is manifestly celebrated by a most rare nobleness in the ways of the clouds, the colours of the woods, the glitter of the waters, yet on earth all has been as it was wont to be?

So far, the life of men moving to and fro across the bridges was like the old life that I knew, though, down below, upon the sparkling waters many birds were alighting, or were already seated like wondrous blossoms upon the bulwarks of a barge painted in parrot colours – red and green. When would the entry begin?

In the streets, for the present, the roar continued of the inhuman masses of humanity, amidst which a child's crying for a toy was an impertinence, a terrible pretty interruption of the violent moving swoon. Between the millions and the one no agreement was visible. The wind summoned the colour in a girl's cheeks. There, one smiled with inward bliss. Another talked serenely with lovely soft mouth and wide eyes that saw only one other pair as the man next her bent his head nearer. The wind wagged the tails of blue or brown fur about the forms of luxurious tall women, and poured wine into their bodies, so that their complexions glowed under their violet hats. But in one moment the passing loveliness of spirit, or form, or gesture, sank and was drowned in the oceanic multitude. A boy had just met his father at a railway station, and was glad; he held the man's hand, and was trotting gently, trying to get him to run – he failed: then in delight put his arm to his father's waist and was carried along thus, half lifted from the ground, for several yards, smiling and chattering like a bird on a waving branch. The two obstructed others, who took a step to left or right in disdain or impatience. Only a child at an alley entrance saw and laughed, wishing she were his sister, and had his father. A moment, and these also were swallowed up.

I came to broader pavements. Here was less haste; and women went in and out of the crowd, not only parallel to the street, but crosswise here and there; and a man could go at any pace, not of necessity the crowd's. Some of the most beautiful civilized women of the world moved slowly and musically in an intricate pattern, which any one could watch freely; they had a background of lustrous jewellery, metal-work and glass, gorgeous cloths and silks, and many had a foil in the stiff black and white male figures beside them. They moved without fear. Stately, costly, tender, beautiful, nevertheless, though so near, they were seen as in a magic crystal that enshrines the remote and the long dead. They walked as in dream, regardlessly smiling. They cast their proud or kind eyes hither and thither. Once in the intense light of a jeweller's shop, spangled with pearls, diamonds, and gold, a large red hand, cold and not quite clean, appeared from within, holding in three fearful, careful fingers a brooch of gold and diamonds, which it placed among the others, and then withdrew itself slowly, tremulously, lest it should work harm to those dazzling cressets. The eyes of the women watched the brooch: the red hand need not have been so fearful; it was unseen – the soul was hid. Straight through the women, in the middle of the broad pavement, and very slowly, went an old man. He was short, and his patched overcoat fell in a parallel-ogram from his shoulders almost to the pavement. From underneath his little cap massive gray curls sprouted and spread over his upturned collar. Just below the fringe of his coat his bare heels glowed red. His hands rested deep in his pockets. His face was almost concealed by curls and collar: all that showed itself was the glazed cold red of his cheeks and large, straight nose, and the glitter of grey eyes that looked neither to left nor to right, but ahead and somewhat down. Not a sound did he make, save the flap of rotten leather against feet which he scarcely raised lest the shoes should fall off. Doubtless the composer of the harmonies of this day could have made use of the old man – doubtless he did; but as it was a feast day of the gods, not of men, I did not understand. Around this figure, clad in complete hue of poverty, the dance of women in violet and black, cinnamon and green, tawny and gray, scarlet and slate, and the browns and golden browns of animals' fur, wove itself fantastically. The dance heeded him not, nor he the dance. The sun shone bright. The wind blew and waved the smoke and the flags wildly against the sky. The horses curved their stout necks, showing their teeth, trampling, massing head by head in rank and cluster, a frieze as magnificent as the procession of white clouds gilded, rolling along the horizon. (*In Pursuit of Spring*, 10–14)

'Hampstead Heath in August – London Miniatures'

Hampstead Heath is too good in itself to be made or obliterated by associations. When you have gone up nearly to the top of Heath Street – put in a certain humour by oldish, quiet shops, and flagged pavement in place of asphalte – you forget Keats and Leigh Hunt, 'Arry and 'Arriet and Mr Kipling. The street goes steep and straight up to perhaps the highest point of the heath, and when you are almost there the walls of the last pair of houses frame the milky blue of the high harvest sky. Then, suddenly, they seem the last houses in the world; for only a hundred yards of ground lies visible between you and the sky.

This patch, containing a pond, is of hard, dry, bare, undulating gravel like a sea beach, and because nothing is to be seen beyond it save the unclouded blue, it creates instantly and powerfully the belief that beyond the edge of this beach the sea is hidden, whether at the foot of a cliff or of a gradual slope is uncertain. The belief lasts a quarter of a minute, and once at the top of the street and on this bare patch, the horizon is seen to be not a curve of sea, but serrated woods upon a long line of hills, all swiftly revealed as if by a miraculous command at blast of trumpet. Almost in the same moment, over the edge, the hollow land of the heath appears below you. Houses unmistakably bound it. Sometimes they look over it as if they regarded it as a possession. Sometimes as if they felt some dull aston-ishment at being separated only by the road from these billowy trees and wild hollows.

Were the heath level, this sense of possession would be lasting and complete. But the uneven wildness due to nature and excavation makes up for its small extent and saves the heath from the humiliation. Thus the houses are nothing but a frame: they do not combine the heath; they neither influence it nor receive any influence from it. They stand bald and impotent at the edge of this fragment of the wild. They are indifferent to the dry air, spiced with harvest, which divides all the little leaves of the trees and carries bright notes of swallows and scattering linnets.

The last sheet but one of August Bank Holiday paper has been picked up. The dust, though harsh to feet and eyes and nostrils and fingers, is sweet to the mind because it is the dust of summer, and the linnets sweeten it like a fount breaking out of dry sand. This wind, thought soft as sleep, is one of the great winds of the world: it touches the cheek with the tip of a light wing dipped in coolness, though the air is as as fiery as it should be at St. Bartholomew-tide. It is no mere afterthought from the first illusion of distant sea: this August air extends from sea to sea over the world, linking the streets and these suburb glades to the upland corn, leagues beyond league, and to the waves shim-mering around the coast. (*The Last Sheaf*, 79–81)

The turf in Richmond Park atones for the walls and fences, the gates, the keepers, the regulations, the Royal residence. Wimbledon Common, where everyone can do practically as he pleases, day and night, and where nearly everybody does, has nothing like this turf. Any son of man, I believe, except a gipsy following his profession, or a naked savage, is admitted into Richmond Park, and yet nowhere has the grass disappeared or become mangy; even well-used paths are still green.

This is due to the fact that there is a Presence always in the park. No doubt this Presence will be explained away by some who believe in the omnipotence of Royalty, deer, and entrance gates; but these things do not wholly explain it, either for Royalist or Republican. The dignity and perfection of these few miles of open country are as repellent to some as they are attractive to others: no one will deny the Presence.

The combination here of the uncultivated and the refined is a beautiful one. Nothing could be purer and freer than the long clear levels, the flowing gradual rises of rushy and ferny turf – the buff oak-woods on the higher places, with clean-curved borderings of bracken – the companies of glowing beeches or elms here and there, and of crimsoned hawthorns, big and old, like those in Savernake Forest, – often to be seen without one human visitor, while the green woodpecker laughs astonishingly, and the stags fence and roar under the trees. Yet nothing, to experienced eyes, could be more plainly due to refinement, depending on generations of forethought and protection, and judicious neglect.

Few can complain of the enclosures which preserve

thickets in untouched abundance. They are to the park what the park is to the outer world. They are citadels of quiet. Their palings give opportunities for adventures to the adventurous: for the rest there is the pleasure of looking in on these secret, secluded little provinces, all the sweeter for being out of reach, except of the mind, and of the squirrels and the birds, the pied chaffinches chinking all through the November day as they flit, the single thrush, singing his mild November song in the poplar that has four yellow leaves left at its point, the robin mysteriously warbling, mysteriously silent, mysteriously rustling among the dead leaves.

Richmond Park has all the qualities of other parks, the unploughed undulations, the old trees, irregularly but happily scattered, the winding, well-kept roads, the cloistered wilderness, the deer, the squirrels, the jackdaws, the notice-boards; but they appear to be in greater perfection, because the walls keep in the deer and the peace, but keep out London. Of course, they keep out other things, so that in a sense the park is only half real, as if it were under a glass-case. Without the glass-case, however, it could not exist; it would be destroyed by the life which it now excludes or converts. (*The Last Sheaf*, 83–6)

'Harrow-on-the-Hill in December'

Far away and high up the sky of morning is blue, its clouds are white, but under them travels a loose, dirty scud, letting fall momentary showers at intervals. The earth glimmers with myriads of little pools; the trees are very black, and the green and gold of moss is bright among the branches. In the shadowy and nevertheless clear air, under the ghost of a moon, thrushes are singing with sharp voices. They seem to sing away the drift and the showers, and presently all the sky is pure except for a procession of mountainous clouds along the horizon, having grey sides and snowy summits, which are obliterated southwards by the December sun in a blaze of white; and Harrow-on-the-Hill, and St. Mary's hilltop spire among its elms and lime-trees, stand up hard and bold in the midst of a land gleaming with innumerable pastures, interlaced and bounded by dark trees that were many of them not young when Byron looked out over them from Peachey's grave in the churchyard. As for London, it is a pale and silent conjectural city under that misty blaze of the sun. Looking away from London across the spread of country which a straight railway instead of a winding river pierces, hardly a house is visible until after the eye has returned from the distance and condescended to look just below, beyond the foot of this green hill. There lie the villas of Harrow – the dairy-farms among their elms and horse-chestnuts – Roxeth village, with its plain old cottages, a gasometer, and a small inn called 'The Timber Carriage,' belonging, I suppose, to the period of the tomb in St. Mary's, where John Henry North, a judge of the Admiralty in Ireland, 'without a superior in chaste and classic eloquence in Parliament,'[38] lies buried. That wide country of elm and oak still needs timber carriages, if not chaste and classic eloquence in Parliament. For eastwards rank beyond rank of round-topped trees, on land gently rising to the horizon, combine into one wood, streaked by a few strips of meadow. And there absolutely not one house can be seen. A solitary crow steers for it: he sinks among the trees with a croak as if he were the only being alive in all that woodland. The houses immediately about me and the nearness of London are not merely powerless for the moment to spoil the solitude of this crow's landscape at fall of night: they intensify the unexpected solitude, because they make it seem improbable, fantastical. But it does not pass away or change; it becomes part of the deep night of many stars, while the houses themselves are unreal, hollow, transitory things, and London a foreign city of ghosts. (*The Last Sheaf*, 86–8)

'Kew Gardens in January'

On an ordinary crowded afternoon the gardens at Kew are like a museum of all the trees and plants written by the Creator. There is something incongruous and intrusive in the rustle of leaves and the song of birds, something awkwardly and astonishingly unofficial in a shower of real rain. But in January the trees rebel: they refuse to admit that they are safe-locked in a museum. They are no longer self-conscious and peaceful about their labels. The Scotch fir forgets that the heather was planted at his feet by order. The silver lime has lost her shyness of the fact that in summer she has one low small branch where all the leaves are three times the normal size – next year perhaps it will be different. The deciduous trees seem glad to have cast off their best clothes that used to make them quite at ease with the pretty dresses of ladies strolling amongst them. With their naked boughs, dark and hard, they utter wintry noises as if they formed a conspiracy to act the parts of trees at liberty – as if the beeches were among a thousand companions on the steep slope of a down, the elms out in an undulating meadow in a friendly cluster, and the ash-trees overhanging a mountain roadside. The birds haunting them are also freer today, when the west wind is mild and the sun gentle in a bower of grey clouds. The whistle of the nuthatch, solitary in the top branches, makes the elms happy. The ash is flattered by the great tit that hangs so low on its twigs, saying 'Chittabob,' and then over and over again, 'I'll wait a bit … I'll wait'. The beech knows well that it is right for a green wood-pecker to rush laughing loudly into its arms. When the fir has a band of starlings piping together on its crest it is an exile no longer. The hawthorn has its bullfinch and is comforted. The bold challenging song of a missel-thrush [mistle thrush] persuades all but the palms that the tropical glass-house is an illusion which must fade when the sunlight ceases to glitter on it. Today the grassy glades are not mere straight green streets. They have a wildness, completed by a light and already half-melted fall of snow. They would not resent a Gypsy camp and camp fire in place of a nursemaid and silken children. They lead the eye out to a sunset sky as yellow as silk in the cocoon, or down to the Thames where willows are blowing and the water is rippled all over like a file. Today the river is not, as it sometimes is, a rude contrast to the ordered gardens, but it gives another touch, like the west wind, the clouded sky, and the birds singing, to the liberty of the winter trees. When I have gone out and the gates are closed, the conspirators are silent, dark, and happy in the twilight, as if they were thoroughly assured that with the night all will be well with them, and their dreams are to be confirmed for ever. (*The Last Sheaf*, 88–90)

Oxford

At sunset or at dawn the city's place in the world, as a beautiful thing, is clearest. Few cities look other than sad at those hours; many, unless hid in their own smoke, look cheap. Oxford becomes part of the magic of sunset and dawn, – is, as it were, gathered into the bosom of the power that is abroad. Yet, if it is one with the hills and the clouds and the silence, the human dignity of the place is also significant. The work of the ancient architect conspires with that of the sunset and of long, pregnant tracts of time; and I know not whether to thank, for the beauty of the place, its genius or perhaps the divinest series of accidents that have ever agreed to foster the forward-looking designs of men. In the days when what is admirable in Oxford was built, the builder made no pretence to please his neighbour. He made what he loved. In many cases he was probably indifferent to everything else. But the genius of the place took care; and only the recent architects who have endeavoured to work in harmony with the place have failed. There is a gentle and puissant harmonising influence in Oxford which nothing can escape. I am no lover of Georgian architecture and am often blind to the power of Wren; but in Oxford I have no such incapacities; and I believe that here architecture should be judged, not as Norman or classical, as the work of Wolsey or Aldrich, but as Oxford architecture. The library at Christ Church, or any other work of the eighteenth century, seems to me as divine a thing, though as yet it lacks the complete unction of antiquity, as Mob Quad at Merton or Magdalen Tower. To pass from the Norman work of St. Peter's in the East to the Palladianism of Peckwater quadrangle, is but to descend from one to another of the same honourable race. If certain extremely new edifices wear out a thousand years they will probably be worthy of reverence at the end of that time, and be in harmony with Merton chapel and Balliol hall at once. Nothing is so deserving, few things so exacting, of respect, from transitory men as age. Things change, and improvements are questioned or questionable; but, for me, age is as good as an improvement; and Oxford honours what is old with particular dignities and graces; under her influence the work of age is at once blander and more swift.

But this gentle tyranny, – as of the Mother of Christ, who, in Leonardo's picture, unites angel and holy child and St. John with outspread hands, – is exerted not only upon the stones, but also upon the people of the place. A man may at Oxford rejoice in the company of another whom it is a self-sacrifice to meet elsewhere. He finds himself marvelling that one who was merely a gentleman in London can be interesting in Long Wall Street or on the Cherwell. The superb, expensive young man who thinks that there is 'practically nobody in Oxford' – the poor, soiled scholar – the exuberant, crimson-lipped athlete, whose stride is a challenge, his voice a trumpet call – the lean and larded aesthete, busily engaged upon the quaint designs of oriental life, – all discover some point in common when they are seen together in the Schools, or on the riverside. (From 'On Entering Oxford', *Oxford*, 5–7)

'Swansea Village' (extract)

I do not go [to Swansea] because they will tell me those brand-new edifices are on the site of the old block-cottages 'where the bad women lived' – as if the 'bad women' were used in the foundations or had been scared out of their iniquity by the splendours of architecture. The pleasant accidents are many in Swansea. The docks are always pleasant with the smell of tar, the weaving whirl of seagulls and the still ships, the cold green water reflecting the gaudy figurehead of the *Kate*, the men unloading potatoes, the painter slung under the bowsprit with a fag in his mouth, which he puts behind his ear to whistle 'Away to Rio'. For that minute the ship looks like a beautiful great captive beast, beautiful in the same manner as the neighbouring caged thrush's song of pure thickets, the sun, the wind, and the rain. I like, too, the rag-and-bone man blowing one deep note on his horn as he travels mean streets; and the cockle-women (their white scoured cockle-tubs on their heads or under their arms) from Penclawdd, dressed in half a dozen thicknesses of flannel, striped and checked, all different and all showy – with broad hips, no waists, stout legs slowly and powerfully moving, and the clearest of complexions and brightest of lips and eyes under their fine soft brown hair. Six days of the week I like the whole Swansea crowd of factory men and girls, the shawled mothers, the seamen, the country folk, though not one element is exceptionally picturesque.

These pleasant and unpleasant things, however, have little to do with the final effect, composite but very definite, of the whole town: they colour certain days, but no more. What counts most is the careless, graceless nature of Swansea, its lordly assemblage of chimney-stacks, its position at a river mouth between mountains, and the neighbourhood of sea. Cheapness, *clapham-junction,* squalor, or actual hideousness is everywhere in contrast with grandeur, and even sublimity, and these qualities do not alternate, but conflict, or in some way co-operate. In the central streets, broad and glassy, thronged to the point of tumult with men and beasts and every kind of vehicle; in the outward-going roads of monotonous, and dismal or unclean, cottages, threaded by electric trams and country carts, and in sunless courts where privacy and publicity are one, you have always in sight either sea or mountain. (*The Last Sheaf,* 153–54)

New Developments – London

It is easier to like the blackbird's shrubbery, the lawn, the big elm, or oak, and the few dozen fruit trees, of the one or two larger and older houses surviving – for example, at the top of Burntwood Lane. The almond, the mulberry, the apple trees in these gardens have a menaced or actually caged loveliness, as of a creature detained from some world far from ours, if they are not, as in some cases they are, the lost angels of ruined paradises.

Burntwood Lane, leading down from a residential district to an industrial district, is no longer as pretty as its name. Also, when it seems to be aiming at the country, it turns into a street of maisonettes, with a vista of houses terminated by the two tall red chimneys of the Wimbledon Electricity Works. But it has its character. The Lunatic Asylum helps it with broad, cultivated squares, elms, and rooks' nests, and the voices of cows and pigs behind the railings that line it on the left hand from top to bottom. On the right, playfields waiting to be built all over give it a lesser advantage. How sorry are the unprotected elms on that side! They will never be old. Man, child, and dog, walking in and out of them, climbing them, kicking and cutting them, have made them as little like trees as it is possible for them to be while they yet live. They have one hour of prettiness, when the leaf-buds are as big as peas on the little side sprays low down. Then on a Saturday – or on a Sunday, when the path is darkened by adults in their best clothes – the children come and pick the sprays in bunches instead of primroses. For there are no primroses, no celandines, no dandelions outside the fences in Burntwood Lane. And Garratt Green at the bottom is now but a railed-in, perfectly level square for games, with rules on a notice-board. It is greener than when it was crossed diagonally by paths, and honoured on a Saturday by gypsies and coco-nut-shies. Probably it now gives some satisfaction to the greatest number possible, but nobody will ever again, until *After London*, think of Garratt Green as a sort of country place. I went round it and its footballers in haste. Nor is that thickening portion of London beyond it easily made to appear beautiful or interesting. It is flat and low, suitable rather for vegetables than men, and built on chiefly because people can always be enticed into new houses. The flatter and lower and more suitable for vegetables, the more easily satisfied are the people with their houses, partly because they are poor, partly because they are half country folk and like this kind of land, it may be, and the river Wandel, the watercress beds, the swampy places, the market gardens, the cabbages and lavender, and Mitcham Fair, more than they would like the church-parade along Bolingbroke Grove, the bands, the teetotallers, the athe-ists, and the tennis-players, on the commons which have a gravel soil. (*In Pursuit of Spring*, 36–9)

Walking through London Suburbs

The hundreds of streets parallel or at angles with the railway – some exposing flowery or neglected back gardens, bedrooms half seen through open windows, pigeon houses with pigeons bowing or flashing in flight, all manner of domesticities surprised – others a line of shop fronts and gorgeous or neat or faded women going to and fro – others, again, a small space that had been green and was still grassy under its encumbrance of dead trees, scaffolding and bricks – some with inns having good names – these streets are the strangest thing in the world. They have never been discovered. They cannot be classified. There is no tradition about them. Poets have not shown how we are to regard them. They are to us as mountains were in the Middle Ages, sublime, difficult, immense; and yet so new that we have inherited no certain attitude towards them, of liking or dislike. They suggest so much that they mean nothing at all. The eye strains at them as at Russian characters which are known to stand for something beautiful or terrible; but there is no translator: it sees a thousand things which at the moment of seeing are significant, but they obliterate one another. More than battlefield or library, they are dense with human life. They are as multitudinous and painful and unsatisfying as the stars. They propose themselves as a problem to the mind, only a little less so at night when their surfaces hand the mind on to the analogies of sea waves or large woods.

Nor at the end of my journey was the problem solved. It was a land of new streets and half-built streets and devastated lanes. Ivied elm trunks lay about with scaffold poles, uprooted shrubs were mingled with bricks, mortar with turf, shining baths and sinks and rusty fire grates with dead thistles and thorns. Here and there a man in a silk hat or a little girl with neat ankles and high brown boots stepped amidst the deeply rutted mud. An artist who wished to depict the Fall and some sympathy with it in the face of a ruined Eden might have had little to do but copy an acre of the surviving fields.

A north wind swept the land clean. In the hedges and standing trees, it sobbed at intervals like a bitter child forcing himself to cry; in the windowless houses it made a merrier sound like a horn. It drove workmen and passers-by to spend as much time as possible in 'The King's Head' and there the medley of the land was repeated. Irish and Cockney accents mingled with Kentish; American would not have been out of place. No one seemed to dislike the best room in the inn, where there was a piano, a coloured picture of Lord Roberts and of the landlord as a youth, an old print of snipe-shooting, some gaudy and fanciful advertisements of spirits, and no fire to warm the wall-paper which had once had a pattern characteristic of poor bathrooms. (*The Heart of England*, 3–5)

'The New House' (March 1915, *Last Poems*)

> Now first, as I shut the door,
>   I was alone
> In the new house; and the wind
>   Began to moan.
>
> Old at once was the house,
>   And I was old;
> My ears were teased with the dread
>   Of what was foretold,
>
> Nights of storm, days of mist, without end;
>   Sad days when the sun
> Shone in vain: old griefs and griefs
>   Not yet begun.
>
> All was foretold me; naught
>   Could I foresee;
> But I learned how the wind would sound
>   After these things should be.

Letchworth Garden City

After a road from a level crossing had come in on the left, I kept straight on along the right side of a hedge dividing the railway from a big field, and past the left edge of a shallow chalk pit. There was no road here, but several tracks went through the long grass, and mistake was impossible. On the right two paths went off to some of the new houses of the Letchworth Garden City, and to a building gigantically labelled 'IDRIS'. This was, I suppose, the temple of this city's god, though the name, except as the Welsh equivalent for Arthur, was unknown to me. They say now that Arthur was a solar hero, and when in doubt men might do worse than to worship the sun, if they could discover how. At Letchworth they were endeavouring to do so. The sun was not benign or even merciful in return for these efforts. He responded by telling the truth with his most brilliant beams, so that the city resembled a caravan of bathing machines, except that there was no sea and the machines could not conveniently be moved. At the end of the big field I crossed a new road and entered among the elders and thorn trees of the edge of Norton Common. Here there were several parallel paths, and on the left behind a hedge was a garden-city street called 'Icknield Way'. This represented the line of the road, but whether this or the path on the other side of the hedge was more on the old course I cannot say. Past the houses 'Icknield Way' ceased to be a road fit for perambulators and became a rough track, chiefly used for carrying building materials. It followed along a hedge and past a sand pit, in one place a little hollowed out. It was miserable with the rank grass of newly 'developed' districts. After a road came in from under the railway on the left, it began to curve away north and leave the railway. Once more it was between hedges; but with all its vicissitudes it had remained a parish boundary all the way from Slip Inn Hill near Odsey. It was going uphill, and presently I could see not only the corn, sainfoin, and houses growing round about, but in the south-west the line of hedged and wooded hills above Ippollitts, Offley, and Pirton. Letchworth was still in sight, like so many wounds on the earth and so much sticking-plaster. But, though behind me, it was fascinating, like all these raw settlements. It is a curious pleasure to see them besieged by docks and nettles, and, as sometimes happens, quietly overcome by docks and nettles. They look new until suddenly they are unvenerably old. Letchworth may turn out to be an exception, but as I hurried through it, some back gardens, some forlorn new roads, and the tune of 'She's off with the wraggle-taggle gipsies, oh!' sent my thoughts mysteriously but irresistibly to the desolate new-old settlements I have known. (*The Icknield Way*, 124–26)

'Home' (March 1916, *Poems*)

> Fair was the morning, fair our tempers, and
> We had seen nothing fairer than that land,
> Though strange, and the untrodden snow that made
> Wild of the tame, casting out all that was
> Not wild and rustic and old; and we were glad.
>
> Fair, too, was afternoon, and first to pass
> Were we that league of snow, next the north wind
>
> There was nothing to return for, except need,
> And yet we sang nor ever stopped for speed,
> As we did often with the start behind.

Faster still strode we when we came in sight
Of the cold roofs where we must spend the night.
Happy we had not been there, nor could be.
Though we had tasted sleep and food and fellowship
Together long.

   'How quick' to someone's lip
The words came, 'will the beaten horse run home.'

The word 'home' raised a smile in us all three,
And one repeated it, smiling just so
That all knew what he meant and none would say.
Between three counties far apart that lay
We were divided and looked strangely each
At the other, and we knew we were not friends
But fellows in a union that ends
With the necessity for it, as it ought.

Never a word was spoken, not a thought
Was thought, of what the look meant with the word
'Home' as we walked and watched the sunset blurred.
And then to me the word, only the word,
'Homesick,' as it were playfully occurred:
No more.

   If I should ever more admit
Than the mere word I could not endure it
For a day longer: this captivity
Must somehow come to an end, else I should be
Another man, as often now I seem,
Or this life be only an evil dream.

Rural Places – Country Estates

There are parks on both sides of the road, bounded by hedges or high brick walls, and the public road has all the decorum of a drive. For a mile the very ivy which is destined to adorn the goodly wall and spread into forms as grand as those at Godstow Nunnery is protected by wire netting. Doves croon in the oaks: underneath, hazel and birch flicker their new leaves over the pools of bluebells. The swallows fly low over every tuft of the roadside grass and glance into every bay of the wood, and then out above the white road, from which they rebound suddenly and turn, displaying the white rays of their tails. Now and then a gateway reveals the park. The ground undulates, but is ever smooth. It is of the mellow green of late afternoon. Bronzed oak woods bound the undulations, and here and there a solitary tree stands out on the grass and shows its poise and complexity with the added grace of new leaf. The cattle graze as on a painted lawn. A woman in a white dress goes indolent and stately towards the rhododendrons and rook-haunted elms. The scene appears to have its own sun, mellow and serene, that knows not moorland or craggy coast or city. Only a thousand years of settled continuous government, of far-reaching laws, of armies and police, of road-making, of bloody tyranny and tyranny that poisons quietly without blows, could have wrought earth and sky into such a harmony. It is a thing as remote from me here on the dusty road as is the green evening sky and all its tranquility of rose and white, and even more so because the man in the manor house behind the oaks is a puzzle to me, while the sky is always a mystery with which I am content. At such an hour the house and lawns and trees are more wonderfully fortified by the centuries of time than by the walls and gamekeepers. They weave an atmosphere about it. We bow the head and reverence the labour of time in smoothing the grass, mellowing the stone and the manners of the inhabitants, and yet an inevitable conflict ensues in the mind between this respect and the feeling that it is only a respect for surfaces, that a thousand years is a heavy price to pay for the maturing of park and house and gentleman, especially as he is most likely to be a well-meaning parasite on those who are concerned twenty-four hours a day about the difficulty of living and about what to do when they are alive. (*The South Country*, 116–17)

'Haymaking' (July 1915, *Poems*)

> After night's thunder far away had rolled
> The fiery day had a kernel sweet of cold,
> And in the perfect blue the clouds uncurled,
> Like the first gods before they made the world
> And misery, swimming the stormless sea
> In beauty and in divine gaiety.
> The smooth white empty road was lightly strewn
> With leaves – the holly's Autumn falls in June –
> And fir cones standing stiff up in the heat.
> The mill-foot water tumbled white and lit
> With tossing crystals, happier than any crowd
> Of children pouring out of school aloud.
> And in the little thickets where a sleeper
> For ever might lie lost, the nettle-creeper
> And garden warbler sang unceasingly;
> While over them shrill shrieked in his fierce glee
> The swift with wings and tail as sharp and narrow
> As if the bow had flown off with the arrow.
> Only the scent of woodbine and hay new-mown
> Travelled the road. In the field sloping down,
> Park-like, to where its willows showed the brook,

Haymakers rested. The tosser lay forsook
Out in the sun; and the long waggon stood
Without its team, it seemed it never would
Move from the shadow of that single yew.
The team, as still, until their task was due,
Beside the labourers enjoyed the shade
That three squat oaks mid-field together made
Upon a circle of grass and weed uncut,
And on the hollow, once a chalk-pit, but
Now brimmed with nut and elder-flower so clean.
The men leaned on their rakes, about to begin,
But still. And all were silent. All was old,
This morning time, with a great age untold,
Older than Clare and Cobbett, Morland and Crome,
Than, at the field's far edge, the farmer's home,
A white house crouched at the foot of a great tree.
Under the heavens that know not what years be
The men, the beasts, the trees, the implements
Uttered even what they will in times far hence –
All of us gone out of the reach of change –
Immortal in a picture of an old grange.

'The Mill-Water' (July 1915, *Last Poems*)

Only the sound remains
Of the old mill;
Gone is the wheel;
On the prone roof and walls the nettle reigns.

Water that toils no more
Dangles white locks
And, falling, mocks
The music of the mill-wheel's busy roar.

Pretty to see, by day
Its sound is naught
Compared with thought
And talk and noise of labour and of play.

Night makes the difference.
In calm moonlight,
Gloom infinite,
The sound comes surging in upon the sense:

Solitude, company, –
When it is night, –
Grief or delight
By it must haunted or concluded be.

Often the silentness
Has but this one
Companion;
Wherever one creeps in the other is:

Sometimes a thought is drowned
By it, sometimes
Out of it climbs;
All thoughts begin or end upon this sound,

Only the idle foam
Of water falling
Changelessly calling,
Where once men had a work-place and a home.

The Chapel

Close to the village stands a wooded barrow and an ancient
camp; and there are long, flat marches where sea-gulls
waver and mew; and a cluster of oaks so wind-worn that
when a west wind comes it seems to come from them as
they wave their haggish arms; and a little desolate white
church and white-walled graveyard, which on December

evenings will shine and seem to be the only things at one
with the foamy water and the dim sky, before the storm;
and when the storm comes the church is gathered up into
its breast and is a part of it, so that he who walks in the
churchyard is certain that the gods – the gods that grow
old and feeble and die – are there still, and with them all
those phantoms following phantoms in a phantom land, –
a gleam of spears, a murmur of arrows, a shout of victory,
a fair face, a scream of torture, a song, the form of some
conqueror and pursuer of English kings, – which make
Welsh history, so that to read it is like walking in that place
among December leaves that seem never to have lived and
been emerald, and looking at the oaks in the mist, which
are only hollows in the mist, while an ancient wind is cease-
lessly remembering ancient things. (*Beautiful Wales*, 198–99)

'The Mountain Chapel' (December 1914, *Last Poems*)

> Chapel and gravestones, old and few,
> Are shrouded by a mountain fold
> From sound and view
> Of life. The loss of the brook's voice
> Falls like a shadow. All they hear is
> The eternal noise
> Of wind whistling in grass more shrill
> Than aught as human as a sword,
> And saying still:
> ''Tis but a moment since man's birth
> And in another moment more
> Man lies in earth
> For ever; but I am the same
> Now, and shall be, even as I was
> Before he came;
> Till there is nothing I shall be.'
> Yet there the sun shines after noon

So cheerfully
The place almost seems peopled, nor
Lacks cottage chimney, cottage hearth:
It is not more
In size than is a cottage, less
Than any other empty home
In homeliness.
It has a garden of wild flowers
And finest grass and gravestones warm
In sunshine hours
The year through. Men behind the glass
Stand once a week, singing, and drown
The whistling grass
Their ponies munch. And yet somewhere,
Near or far off, there's a man could
Be happy here,
Or one of the gods perhaps, were they
Not of inhuman stature dire,
As poets say
Who have not seen them clearly; if
At sound of any wind of the world
In grass-blades stiff
They would not startle and shudder cold
Under the sun. When gods were young
This wind was old.

NOTES AND REFERENCES

35 'Ladslove' otherwise known as 'old man' (see Thomas's poem by
that name), or 'southern wormwood' (*Artemesia abrotanum*).

36 Joseph Addison, 'Westminster Abbey', *The Spectator*, March 30, 1711.

37 These are made-up names based on the archaic Greek epithets
poluphloisbos (meaning 'much-resounding', from Homer) and
acromatos (meaning 'colourless', from Plato).

38 A quote from John Henry North's memorial epitaph in St Mary's
Church, Harrow on the Hill, London.

Chapter Eight

The Seasons and the Weather

Some of Thomas's early poems, including 'November', 'March' and 'October', are suggestive of British folk weather rhymes, such as 'red sky at night, shepherd's delight' and 'thunder before seven, rain before eleven', and these had long served as a form of weather forecast. Many folk weather rhymes are actually surprisingly accurate. And yet a poet's (and especially this poet's) relationship to the weather is bound to be complex. For Thomas, the weather rhymes made him reflect on the differences between humans and the rest of nature. 'October' shows the speaker attempting to understand his own 'inner weather' through nature – here harebell, scabious, tormentil, blackberry, birch, fern and gorse. Thomas described the plant life of the grassland and heath of the Hampshire Weald in the autumn and at the same time he communicated what this rich scene felt like.

We have already seen that in *In Pursuit of Spring* Thomas was aware how we see the outer world is conditioned by our state of mind. In the extract about the 'Red Brick House' Thomas described how an experience of beauty alone was not enough to induce happiness. In 'Wind and Mist', (and 'The New House', see Chapter Seven) he recalled how the wind, mist and rain he encountered in another house exacerbated his negative moods. The poem 'Rain', and the related extract from *The Icknield Way*, show how Thomas's melancholy could either be alleviated or worsened by the weather. In the extracts from *In Pursuit of Spring*, Thomas explained that what he was looking for was a combination of inner and outer inspiration. The inner inspiration – itself a kind of 'spring' – came from his friendship with the American poet Robert Frost which showed him he could write poetry. The outer inspiration always came from the natural environment but he felt there could be no 'nature cure' without a change in our inner weather. Only then could it be said of Edward Thomas that, like his fictional poet, Rhys (below), 'he loved sun, rain, and wind, separately and all together'.

The Seasons – A House through the Seasons

All other houses that I have known, beautiful, plain, dear, hateful, or dull, have been somehow subdued and made spiritual houses in course of time and of memory. The Red Brick House is the only unconquerable one. To this day it remains a body, and dead. Its fires are black grates that burnt coal. Its walls are wall-paper in strips at a certain price. Its garden is still mere hard ground to be dug (and to grow chiefly the inexorable couch grass). I saw a beautiful spring come into the world from that house: spring passed down the elms on the opposite side of the road, led one morning by a wryneck screaming loud in the tops of the trees. Pewits came to the ploughed field beyond, and tossed in the sunny wind, as I would have done in such days of March, had I been a bird. Beautiful autumn, beautiful spring, beautiful summer, triumphed round about that building. Many days can I remember from those seasons, a February day, for example – a pale morning after a night of lashing rain, a pale, still morning. The puddles, the ruts of the cartways, the smooth surface of the winding roads, glistened in the brown, ploughed world. The Downs were clear and dark and hard under a silver-clouded blue sky, and far beyond them were the upper ridges of small mountainous clouds of a yellowish and sunlit white. Very sombre were the woods. Each thing was dark or bright; all was fresh and cold. Suddenly a bee twanged through the air to a snowdrop on the south side of the Red Brick House. Inside the house a subtle devil was refusing to let a soul enter into its walls – a subtle but a bodiless and soulless devil, negative and denying. During the nine years since it was built eight families had sojourned in the house, and had not given it a soul; nor had the several intervals of vacancy given it a ghost.

Sometimes death will give a soul to a house. I once saw the soul of a dead man given to a new little house with a verandah. The swifts were racing to and fro between the rows of new houses. They flew just above the level of men's hats, except when they turned with a rapier-like twist up into the air. While they raced they screamed continually shrill screams of a fierce hilarity. There were half a hundred of them all flying as upon the surface of an invisible stream surmounted by a few black, bobbing hats, or, very rarely, an upturned white face; and no part of the streets was for more than a second without a crescent black wing and a shriek. They had taken possession of the town. Under their rush and cry the people in the streets were silent, walking blankly and straight ahead, and all looking old in contrast with the tumultuous and violent youth of the birds. The thought came into my head as I was passing the last of the houses that even so must the birds have been racing and screaming when the Danes harried this way a thousand years ago, and thus went they over the head of Dante in the streets of Florence. In the warriors and in the poet there was a life clearly and mightily akin to that in the bird's throat and wing, but here all was grey, all was dead. (*The Icknield Way*, 166–68)

'Wind and Mist' (April 1915, *Last Poems*)

They met inside the gateway that gives the view,
A hollow land as vast as heaven. 'It is
A pleasant day, sir.' 'A very pleasant day.'
'And what a view here. If you like angled fields
Of grass and grain bounded by oak and thorn,
Here is a league. Had we with Germany
To play upon this board it could not be
More dear than April has made it with a smile.
The fields beyond that league close in together
And merge, even as our days into the past,
Into one wood that has a shining pane
Of water. Then the hills of the horizon –
That is how I should make hills had I to show
One who would never see them what hills
    were like.'
'Yes. Sixty miles of South Downs at one glance.
Sometimes a man feels proud at them, as if
He had just created them with one mighty
    thought.'
'That house, though modern, could not be better
    planned
For its position. I never liked a new
House better. Could you tell me who lives in it?'
'No one.' 'Ah – and I was peopling all
Those windows on the south with happy eyes,
The terrace under them with happy feet;
'Girls – ' 'Sir, I know. I know. I have seen that
    house
Through mist look lovely as a castle in Spain,
And airier. I have thought: "'Twere happy there
To live." And I have laughed at that

Because I lived there then.' 'Extraordinary.'
'Yes, with my furniture and family
Still in it, I, knowing every nook of it
And loving none, and in fact hating it.'
'Dear me! How could that be? But pardon me.'
'No offence. Doubtless the house was not to
    blame,
But the eye watching from those windows saw,
Many a day, day after day, mist – mist
Like chaos surging back – and felt itself
Alone in all the world, marooned alone.
We lived in clouds, on a cliff's edge almost
(You see), and if clouds went, the visible earth
Lay too far off beneath and like a cloud.
I did not know it was the earth I loved
Until I tried to live there in the clouds
And the earth turned to cloud.' 'You had a
    garden
Of flint and clay, too.' 'True; that was real enough.
The flint was the one crop that never failed.
The clay first broke my heart, and then my back;
And the back heals not. There were other things
Real, too. In that room at the gable a child
Was born while the wind chilled a summer dawn:
    Never looked grey mind on a greyer one
Than when the child's cry broke above the
    groans.'
'I hope they were both spared.' 'They were.
    Oh yes.
But flint and clay and childbirth were too real
For this cloud-castle. I had forgot the wind.
Pray do not let me get on to the wind.
You would not understand about the wind.

It is my subject, and compared with me
Those who have always lived on the firm ground
Are quite unreal in this matter of the wind.
There were whole days and nights when the wind
     and I
Between us shared the world, and the wind ruled
And I obeyed it and forgot the mist.
My past and the past of the world were in the wind.
Now you may say that though you understand
And feel for me, and so on, you yourself
Would find it different. You are all like that
If once you stand here free from wind and mist:
     I might as well be talking to wind and mist.
You would believe the house-agent's young man
Who gives no heed to anything I say.
Good morning. But one word. I want to admit
That I would try the house once more, if I could;
As I should like to try being young again.'

Spring – 'Thaw' (March 1916, *Poems*)

Over the land freckled with snow half-thawed
The speculating rooks at their nests cawed
And saw from elm-tops, delicate as flower of
     grass,
What we below could not see, Winter pass.

'Like the Touch of Rain' (April 1916, *Poems*)

Like the touch of rain she was
On a man's flesh and hair and eyes
When the joy of walking thus
Has taken him by surprise:

With the love of the storm he burns,
He sings, he laughs, well I know how,
But forgets when he returns
As I shall not forget her 'Go now.'

Those two words shut a door
Between me and the blessed rain
That was never shut before
And will not open again.

Summer – 'One Swallow Doesn't Make a Summer'

There was a poet in North Wales long ago named Rhys, who loved April because he loved sun, rain, and wind, separately and all together. As soon as April came he began to write poems saying why April was better than March and May. One year, however, he cut his hand so badly in a briar bush by the river Alun that he could not write, yet he was sure that the poem which he had made in his head on the first of April was better than any he had ever written down. He had found a swallow at the edge of the river, dead, killed by a hawk. First he had cried over the swallow. Then the sun had come out, and he made the poem. He had tried hard to write it down with his left hand, using a quill from the dead swallow's wing, dipping it in the blood of his wounded right hand. But he was too impatient. The first verse looked very bad, written slowly and awkwardly with the left hand, and he threw it angrily into the water. He had made up his mind what to do.

He went to a monk, an old man, and asked him to take down the poem from his dictation, though he knew in his heart that the poem was so good he never would forget it. The monk did as he was asked, but Rhys left the poem with him in order that it might be copied out at leisure in his best handwriting and sent to the prince.

That night Rhys was taken ill; before he had seen another swallow he was dead. His last message was that the poem should be carried to the prince.

Now, the monk hated poems, and especially those that were written in Welsh instead of in Latin. And Rhys's poem seemed to him the most foolish poem that was ever written, even in Welsh, because every verse said that dead swallow had brought the Summer on its wings and that now, since the bird was dead, Summer could not escape from Wales. This was ridiculous, it was a lie, said the monk. Summer was not a thing, said he. Besides, he added, Summer will come to all the world, and not Wales only. Had this Swallow brought it from land to land, he asked. Moreover, he sneered, not a thousand swallows can make Summer if it is wet and cold. For this reason, and also because he hoped that he might have the poet's place of honour with the prince, the monk destroyed the poem, and wrote a very bad one of his own.

The monk's poem was contrary to Rhys's; at the end of every verse were these words; 'One swallow doesn't make a summer'. It pleased him so much that he sent it to the prince.

But the prince loved Rhys. When the monk's poem arrived he was still sorrowing for the poet's death, and the stuff changed his sorrow into anger. 'What bad verses,' he exclaimed, wishing more than ever that he had not lost his poet. The line, 'One swallow doesn't make a summer' particularly enraged him. 'neither does one bad poem make a poet,' he cried, as he gave the manuscript to a goat to eat. The monk was disappointed. Nevertheless, whenever a swallow came in April and bad weather followed, somebody remembered the bad poem and the line: 'One swallow doesn't make a summer'; for the verse that Rhys tossed into the river was lost for ever, and there was nothing left of his poem to prove that the monk was wrong. (*Four and Twenty Blackbirds*, 25–8)

'**May 23**' (February 1915, *Poems*)

> There never was a finer day,
> And never will be while May is May, –
> The third, and not the last of its kind;
> But though fair and clear the two behind
> Seemed pursued by tempests overpast;
> And the morrow with fear that it could not last
> Was spoiled. Today ere the stones were warm
> Five minutes of thunderstorm
> Dashed it with rain, as if to secure,
> By one tear, its beauty the luck to endure.
>
> At mid-day then along the lane
> Old Jack Noman appeared again,
> Jaunty and old, crooked and tall,
> And stopped and grinned at me over the wall,
> With a cowslip bunch in his button-hole
> And one in his cap. Who could say if his roll
> Came from flints in the road, the weather, or ale?
> He was welcome as the nightingale.
> Not an hour of the sun had been wasted on Jack
> 'I've got my Indian complexion back'
> Said he. He was tanned like a harvester,
> Like his short clay pipe, like the leaf and bur
> That clung to his coat from last night's bed,
> Like the ploughland crumbling red.

Fairer flowers were none on the earth
Than his cowslips wet with the dew of their birth,
Or fresher leaves than the cress in his basket.
'Where did they come from, Jack?' 'Don't ask it,
And you'll be told no lies.' 'Very well:
Then I can't buy.' 'I don't want to sell.
Take them and these flowers, too, free.
Perhaps you have something to give me?
Wait till next time. The better the day …
The Lord couldn't make a better, I say;
If he could, he never has done.'
So off went Jack with his roll-walk-run,
Leaving his cresses from Oakshott rill
And his cowslips from Wheatham hill.

'Twas the first day that the midges bit;
But though they bit me, I was glad of it:
Of the dust in my face, too, I was glad.
Spring could do nothing to make me sad.
Bluebells hid all the ruts in the copse.
The elm seeds lay in the road like hops,
That fine day, May the twenty-third,
The day Jack Noman disappeared.

'Bright Clouds' (June 1916, *Poems*)

Bright clouds of may
Shade half the pond.
Beyond,
All but one bay
Of emerald
Tall reeds
Like criss-cross bayonets

Where a bird once called,
Lies bright as the sun.
No one heeds.
The light wind frets
And drifts the scum
Of may-blossom.
Till the moorhen calls
Again
Naught's to be done
By birds or men.
Still the may falls.

Rain

I lay awake listening to the rain, and at first it was as
pleasant to my ear and my mind as it had long been desired;
but before I fell asleep it had become a majestic and finally
a terrible thing, instead of a sweet sound and symbol. It was
accusing and trying me and passing judgment. Long I lay
still under the sentence, listening to the rain, and then at last
listening to words which seemed to be spoken by a ghostly
double beside me. He was muttering: The all-night rain
puts out summer like a torch. In the heavy, black rain fall-
ing straight from invisible, dark sky to invisible, dark earth
the heat of summer is annihilated, the splendour is dead,
the summer is gone. The midnight rain buries it away where
it has buried all sound but its own. I am alone in the dark
still night, and my ear listens to the rain piping in the gutters
and roaring softly in the trees of the world. Even so will the
rain fall darkly upon the grass over the grave when my ears
can hear it no more. I have been glad of the sound of rain,
and wildly sad of it in the past; but that is all over as if it had
never been; my eye is dull and my heart beating evenly and

quietly; I stir neither foot nor hand; I shall not be quieter when I lie under the wet grass and the rain falls, and I of less account than the grass. The summer is gone, and never can it return. There will never be any summer any more, and I am weary of everything. I stay because I am too weak to go. I crawl on because it is easier than to stop. I put my face to the window. There is nothing out there but the blackness and sound of rain. Neither when I shut my eyes can I see anything. I am alone. Once I heard through the rain a bird's questioning watery cry – once only and suddenly. It seemed content, and the solitary note brought up against me the order of nature, all its beauty, exuberance, and everlastingness like an accusation. I am not a part of nature. I am alone. There is nothing else in my world but my dead heart and brain within me and the rain without. Once there was summer, and a great heat and splendour over the earth terrified me and asked me what I could show that was worthy of such an earth. It smote and humiliated me, yet I had eyes to behold it, and I prostrated myself, and by adoration made myself worthy of the splendour. Was I not once blind to the splendour because there was something within me equal to itself? What was it? Love … a name ! … a word ! … less than the watery question of the bird out in the rain. The rain has drowned the splendour. Everything is drowned and dead, all that was once lovely and alive in the world, all that had once been alive and was memorable though dead is now dung for a future that is infinitely less than the falling dark rain. For a moment the mind's eye and ear pretend to see and hear what the eye and ear themselves once knew with delight. The rain denies. There is nothing to be seen or heard, and there never was. Memory, the last chord of the lute, is broken. The rain has been and will be for ever over the earth. There never was anything but the dark rain. Beauty and strength are as nothing to it. Eyes could not flash in it.

I have been lying dreaming until now, and now I have awakened, and there is still nothing but the rain. I am alone. The unborn is not more weak or more ignorant, and like the unborn I wait and wait, knowing neither what has been nor what is to come, because of the rain, which is, has been, and must be. The house is still and silent, and those small noises that make me start are only the imagination of the spirit or they are the rain. There is only the rain for it to feed on and to crawl in. The rain swallows it up as the sea does its own foam. I will lie still and stretch out my body and close my eyes. My breath is all that has been spared by the rain, and that comes softly and at long intervals, as if it were trying to hide itself from the rain. I feel that I am so little I have crept away into a comer and been forgotten by the rain. All else has perished except me and the rain. There is no room for anything in the world but the rain. It alone is great and strong. It alone knows joy. It chants monoton-ous praise of the order of nature, which I have disobeyed or slipped out of. I have done evilly and weakly, and I have left undone. Fool! you never were alive. Lie still. Stretch out yourself like foam on a wave, and think no more of good or evil. There was no good and no evil. There was life and there was death, and you chose. Now there is neither life nor death, but only the rain. Sleep as all things, past, present, and future, lie still and sleep, except the rain, the heavy, black rain falling straight through the air that was once a sea of life. That was a dream only. The truth is that the rain falls for ever and I am melting into it. Black and monotonously sounding is the midnight and solitude of the rain. In a little while or in an age – for it is all one – I shall know the full truth of the words I used to love, I knew

not why, in my days of nature, in the days before the rain:
'Blessed are the dead that the rain rains on'. (*The Icknield Way*, 280–83)

'Rain' (January 1916, *Poems*)

> Rain, midnight rain, nothing but the wild rain
> On this bleak hut, and solitude, and me
> Remembering again that I shall die
> And neither hear the rain nor give it thanks
> For washing me cleaner than I have been
> Since I was born into this solitude.
> Blessed are the dead that the rain rains upon:
> But here I pray that none whom once I loved
> Is dying to-night or lying still awake
> Solitary, listening to the rain,
> Either in pain or thus in sympathy
> Helpless among the living and the dead,
> Like a cold water among broken reeds,
> Myriads of broken reeds all still and stiff,
> Like me who have no love which this wild rain
> Has not dissolved except the love of death,
> If love it be towards what is perfect and
> Cannot, the tempest tells me, disappoint.

Autumn – 'October' (October 1915, *Poems*)

> The green elm with the one great bough of gold
> Lets leaves into the grass slip, one by one, –
> The short hill grass, the mushrooms small
>   milk-white,
> Harebell and scabious and tormentil,
> That blackberry and gorse, in dew and sun,

Bow down to; and the wind travels too light
To shake the fallen birch leaves from the fern;
The gossamers wander at their own will.
At heavier steps than birds' the squirrels scold.

The rich scene has grown fresh again and new
As Spring and to the touch is not more cool
Than it is warm to the gaze; and now I might
As happy be as earth is beautiful,
Were I some other or with earth could turn
In alternation of violet and rose,
Harebell and snowdrop, at their season due,
And gorse that has no time not to be gay.
But if this be not happiness, – who knows?
Some day I shall think this a happy day,
And this mood by the name of melancholy
Shall no more blackened and obscured be.

Winter – 'November' (November 1914, *Poems*)

November's days are thirty:
November's earth is dirty,
Those thirty days, from first to last;
And the prettiest things on ground are the paths
With morning and evening hobnails dinted,
With foot and wing-tip overprinted
Or separately charactered,
Of little beast and little bird.
The fields are mashed by sheep, the roads
Make the worst going, the best the woods
Where dead leaves upward and downward
    scatter.
Few care for the mixture of earth and water,

Twig, leaf, flint, thorn,
Straw, feather, all that men scorn,
Pounded up and sodden by flood,
Condemned as mud.

But of all the months when earth is greener
Not one has clean skies that are cleaner.
Clean and clear and sweet and cold,
They shine above the earth so old,
While the after-tempest cloud
Sails over in silence though winds are loud,
Till the full moon in the east
Looks at the planet in the west
And earth is silent as it is black,
Yet not unhappy for its lack.
Up from the dirty earth men stare:
One imagines a refuge there
Above the mud, in the pure bright
Of the cloudless heavenly light:
Another loves earth and November more dearly
Because without them, he sees clearly,
The sky would be nothing more to his eye
Than he, in any case, is to the sky;
He loves even the mud whose dyes
Renounce all brightness to the skies.

'Lucidity in the Arms of Gloom'

Many days in London have no weather. We are aware only
that it is hot or cold, dry or wet; that we are in or out of
doors; that we are at ease or not. This was not one of them.
Rain lashed and wind roared in the night, enveloping my
room in a turbulent embrace as if it had been a tiny ship in

a great sea, instead of one pigeon-hole in a thousand-fold columbarium[39] deep in London.

Dawn awakened me with its tranquillity. The air was sombrely sweet; there was a lucidity under the gloom of the clouds; the air barely heaved with the ebb of storm; and even when the sun was risen it seemed still twilight. The jangle of the traffic made a wall round about the quiet in which I lay embedded. I scarcely heard the sound of it; but I could not forget the wall. Within the circle of quiet a parrot sang the street songs of twenty years ago very clearly, over and over again, almost as sweetly as a blackbird. I had heard him many times before, but now he sang differently – I did not know or consider how or why. The song was different as the air was. Yet I could not directly feel the air, because the windows were tightly shut against the soot of four neighbouring chimney-stacks.

Out of doors the business and pleasure of the day kept me a close though a moving prisoner. All the morning and afternoon I was glad to see only one thing that was not a human face. It was a portico of high fluted columns rising in a cliff above an expanse of gravel walks and turf. The grey columns were blackened with soot splashes. The grass and the stone were touched with the sweetness that was in the early air and in the bird's song before the rain had dried and the wind quite departed. Both were blessed with the same pure and lovely union of humid coldness, gloom, and lucidity, so that the portico appeared for a moment to be the entrance to halls of unimagined beauty and holiness, as if I should be admitted through them into the cloud-ramparted city of that earlier day. Nevertheless, I found all inside exactly as it had always been; not only the ex-pectation but even the memory of what had fostered it was wiped out without one pause of disappointment. The sunlight, now and then flooding and astonishing the interior, fell through windows that shut out both sky and earth, into an atmosphere incapable of acknowledging the divinity of the rays; they were alien, disturbing, hostile. There was something childish in these displays, so wasteful and passionate, before the spectacled eyes of a number of people reading books in the mummied air of a library.

Once more on this February day, at four in the afternoon, my eyes were unsealed and awakened. The air in the streets of big dark houses was still and hazy, but overhead hung the loftiest sky I had ever seen, and the finest of fine-spun clouds stretched across the pale blue in long white reefs. In a few moments I was again under a roof. This time it was the house of a friend, removed from busy thoroughfares, very silent within. As the old country servant, faintly dingy and sinister, led me up to the usual room, the staircase, and both the shut and the half-seen apartments on either hand, were mysterious and depressing, with something massive and yet temporary, as if in a dream mansion of shadows. Nothing definite was suggested by these doors; anything was possible behind them. Right up to the familiar dark room I always felt the same dull trouble. Then the dim room opened before me: I heard the masterly, kind voice.

It was a high, large room with many corners that I had never explored. The furniture gloomed vaguely above and around the little space that was crossed by our two voices. The long windows were some yards away, and between them and us stood a heavy table, a heavy cabinet, and several chairs. Never had I been to the window and looked out, nor did I today. No lamp was lit. We talked, we were silent, and I was content. Now and then I looked towards the window, which framed only the corner of a house near by, the chimneys of farther houses, and a pallor of sky between and above them. I was aware of the slow stealing away of day. I knew it was slow, and twice I looked at a clock to make sure that I was not being deceived. I was aware also of the beauty of this slow fading. No wind moved, nor was any movement anywhere heard or seen. The stillness and silence were great; the tranquillity was even greater: I dipped into it and shared it while I listened and talked. Several times two or three children passed beneath the window and chattered in loud, shrill voices, but they were unseen. Far from disturbing the tranquillity, the sounds were steeped in it; the silence and stillness of the twilight saturated and embalmed them. But pleasant as in themselves they were entirely, they were far more so by reason of what they suggested.

These voices and this tranquillity spoke of Spring. They told me what an evening it was at home. I knew how the first blackbird was whistling in the broad oak, and, farther away – some very far away – many thrushes were singing in the chill, under the pale light fitly reflected by the faces of earliest primroses. The sound of lambs and of a rookery more distant blended in soft roaring. Underfoot everything was soaked – soaked clay, soaked dead grass; and the land was agleam with silver rain pools and channels. I foresaw tempest of rain and wind on the next day. Perhaps imagination of dark, withered, and sodden land, and the change threatening, helped to perfect that sweetness which was not wholly of earth. The songs of the birds were to cease, and, in their place, blackbirds would be clinking nervously in impenetrable thickets long after sundown, when only a narrowing pane of almost lightless light divided a black mass of cloud from a black horizon. As in the morning streets the essence of the beauty was lucidity in the arms of gloom, so it was now in the clear twilight fields gliding towards black night, tempest, and perhaps a renewal of Winter ... Then a lamp was carried in. The children's voices had gone. In a little while I rose, and, going out, saw precisely that long pane of light that I should have seen low in the west, had I been standing fifty miles off, looking towards Winchester.

Another evening like this one followed. To the south and west of me the Downs were spread out beyond eyesight. Their flowing and quiet lines were an invitation, a temptation. I should have liked to set forth immediately, to travel day and night with that flow and quiet until I reached the nightingale's song, the apple blossom, the perfume of sunny earth. But nothing was more impossible. The next day was sleet. The most I could do was to plan so that perhaps I should find myself travelling in one of those preludes to Summer which are less false than this one. The beautiful Easters I had known came back to me: Easters of five years, twenty years ago; early Easters when the chiffchaff was singing on March 20 in a soft wind; later Easters, when Good Friday brought the swallow, Saturday the cuckoo, Sunday the nightingale. I did not forget Easters of snow and of north wind. In the end I decided to trust to luck – to start on Good Friday on the chance that I should meet fine weather at once or in a day or two. I would go out in that safe, tame fashion, looking for Spring. The date of Easter made nightingales and cuckoos improbable; but I might hope for the chiffchaff, an early martin, some stitchwort blossoms, cuckoo flowers, some larch green, some blackthorn white. I began to think of what the days would be like. Would there be an invisible sky and a coldish wind, yet some ground for hoping, because the blackbirds would be content in their singing at evening, and the dead leaves that trundle in the road would have decreased to a handful? Perhaps there would be another of these dimly promising days. On the third, would the misty morning clear slowly, the Downs barely visible under the low drift, behind which the sky is caked in cloud, with a dirty silver light from the interstices? And would there be one place in this sky which it would be impossible to gaze at, and would this at last become dazzling, would the drift vanish, and the Downs and half the valley be hid in the foundations of a stationary mass of sunlit white cloud? Would the earth begin to crumble in the warm breeze? Would the bees be heard instead of the wind? Would the jackdaws play and cry far up in the pale vault? Would the low east become a region of cumulus clouds, old-ivory-coloured, receding with sunny edges one behind the other infinitely? Would the evening sky be downy-white and clouded softly over the dark copses and the many songs interwoven at seven? Would a clear still night follow, with Lyra and a multitude of stars? (*In Pursuit of Spring*, 16–23)

'March Doubts'

All day the winter seemed to have gone. The horses' hoofs on the moist, firm road made a clear 'cuck-oo' as they rose and fell; and far off, for the first time in the year, a plough-boy, who remembered spring and knew that it would come again, shouted 'Cuckoo! cuckoo!'

A warm wind swept over the humid pastures and red sand-pits on the hills and they gleamed in a lightly muffled sun. Once more in the valleys the ruddy farmhouses and farm-buildings seemed new and fair again, and the oasthouse cones stood up as prophets of spring, since the south wind had turned all their white vanes towards the north, and they felt the sea that lay – an easy journey on such a day – beyond the third or fourth wooded ridge in the south. The leaves of goose-grass, mustard, vetch, dog's mercury, were high above the dead leaves on hedge banks. Primrose and periwinkle were blossoming. Like flowers were the low ash-tree boles where the axe had but lately cut off the tall rods; flowerlike and sweet also the scent from the pits where labourers dipped the freshly peeled ash poles in tar. In the elms, sitting crosswise on a bough, sang thrush and missel [mistle] thrush; in the young corn, the larks; the robins in the thorns; and in all the meadows the guttural notes of the rooks were mellowed by love and the sun.

Making deep brown ruts across the empty green fields came the long waggons piled high with faggots; the wheels rumbled; the harness jingled and shone; the horses panted and the carters cracked their whips.

Soon would the first chiffchaff sing in the young larches; at evening the calm, white, majestic young clouds should lie along the horizon in a clear and holy air; and climbing a steep hill at that hour, the walker should see a window, as it were, thrown open in the sky and hear a music that should silence thought and even regret – as when, on the stage, a window is opened and someone invisible is heard to sing a heavy-laden song below it.

But as I walked and the wind fell for the sunset, the path led me under high, stony beeches. The air was cool and still and moist and waterish dark, and no bird sang. A wood-pigeon spread out his barry tail as he ascended perpendicularly to a hidden place among the branches, and then there was no sound. The waterish half-light seemed to have lasted for ever and to have an eternity ahead. Through the trees a grassy, deeply-rutted road wound downwards, and at the edge the ruts were broad and full of dark water. Still retaining some corruption of the light of the sky upon its surface, that shadowed water gave an immense melancholy to the wood. The reflections of the beeches across it were as the bars of a cage that imprisoned some child of light. It was but a few inches deep of rain, and yet, had it been a legendary pool, or had a drowned woman's hair been stamped into the mud at its edge and left a green forehead exposed, it could not have stained and filled the air more tragically. The cold, the silence, the leaflessness found an expression in that clouded shining surface among the ruts. Life and death seemed to contend there, and I re-called a dream which I had lately dreamed.

I dreamed that someone had cut the cables that anchored me to such tranquillity as had been mine, and that I was drifted out upon an immensity of desolation and solitude. I was without hope, without even the energy of despair that might in time have given birth to hope. But in that desolation I found one business: to search for a poison that should kill slowly, painlessly and unexpect-edly. In that search I lost sight of what had persuaded me to it; yet when at last I succeeded, I took a draught and went out into the road and began to walk. A calm fell upon me such as I had sometimes found in June thunder-storms on lonely hills, or in midnights when I stepped for a moment after long foolish labours to my door, and heard the nightingales singing out from the Pleia-des that overhung the wood, and saw the flower-faced owl sitting on the gate. I walked on, not hastening with a too great desire nor lingering with a too careful quiet-ude. It was as yet early morning, and the wheat sheaves stood on the gentle hills like yellow-haired women kneeling to the sun that was about to rise. Now and then I passed the corners of villages, and sometimes at windows and through doorways, I saw the faces of men and women I had known and seemed to forget, and they smiled and were glad, but not more glad than I. Labouring in the fields also were men whose faces I was happy to recognise and see smiling with recognition. And very sweet it was to go on thus, at ease, knowing neither trouble nor fatigue. I could have gone on, it seemed, for ever, and I wished to live so for ever, when suddenly I remembered the poison. Then of each one I met I begged a remedy. Some reminded me that formerly I had made a poor thing of life, and said that it was too late. Others supposed that I jested. A few asked me to stay with them and rest. The sky and the earth, and the men and women drank of the poison that I had drunken, so that I could not endure the use of my eyes, and I entered a shop to buy some desperate remedy that should end all at once, when, seeing behind the counter a long-dead friend in wedding attire, I awoke.

Even so in the long wet ruts did the false hope of spring contend with the shadows: even so at last did it end, when the dead leaves upon the trees began to stir madly in the night wind, with the sudden, ghastly motion of burnt paper on a still fire when a draught stirs it in a silent room at night; and even the nearest trees seemed to be but fantastic hollows in the misty air. (Chapter VI, 'March Doubts', *The Heart of England*, 38–42)

'Out in the Dark' (*Last Poems*)

Out in the dark over the snow
The fallow fawns invisible go
With the fallow doe;
And the winds blow
Fast as the stars are slow.

Stealthily the dark haunts round
And, when a lamp goes, without sound
At a swifter bound
Than the swiftest hound,
Arrives, and all else is drowned;

And I and star and wind and deer,
Are in the dark together, – near,
Yet far, – and fear
Drums on my ear
In that sage company drear.

How weak and little is the light,
All the universe of sight,
Love and delight,
Before the might,
If you love it not, of night.

NOTES AND REFERENCES

39 A room or building for funeral urns to be stored.

Chapter Nine

Inns and Sleep

Pubs and inns provide physical and mental relief from the process of solitary walking that forms that backbone of Thomas's countryside books. Here you can sample the atmosphere of various early 20th century pubs and inns, and meet their assorted clientele: a Freemason, Old Jack Runaway, a 'coral-lipped' barmaid, a harpist … Sleep can be found in the inn, but so can ale, food, song and other distractions. The extract of Thomas's book *A Literary Pilgrim in England* about Coleridge's poem 'Kubla Khan' is included here because of its connections with Coleridge's dream. Another link can be made, between Coleridge's addiction to opium, the drug of sleep, and Thomas's use of laudanum. As certain passages of Coleridge's poetry may seem to have a hallucinogenic quality, we can sometimes detect a dream-like atmosphere in Thomas's prose (and in 'The Pilgrim', from Chapter Five, Thomas noted this medicine's effects on literary ambition').

'The Trumpet' was inspired by Thomas's time in the Royal Artillery Barracks at Trowbridge, Wiltshire, and describes his adjustment to army life. This followed a process of deliberation that had lasted over a year while he decided whether to enlist (he was over the age of conscription) or to join his friend Robert Frost in America to teach and farm. Thomas became a lance-corporal with the Artists' Rifles, training new recruits in the skills of map reading before seeking this commission, which led him to France in late January 1917. Thomas was killed soon after in the cold April of 1917, when he was a forward observer during the Battle of Arras. 'A Dream' refers both to a dream in which he recalled his time walking with Robert Frost through the meadows of Gloucestershire and the cataclysmic upheavals of the war.

Pubs and Inns – The Inn

The night was dark and solid rain tumultuously invested the inn. As I stood in a dim passage I could see through the bar into the cloudy parlour, square and white, surrounded by settles, each curving about a round table made of one piece of elm on three legs. A reproduction of 'Rent Day' and a coloured picture of a bold Spanish beauty hung on the wall, which, for the rest, was sufficiently adorned by the sharp shadows of men's figures and furniture that mingled grotesquely. All the men but one leaned back upon the settles or forward upon the tables, their hands on their tankards, watching the one who sang a ballad – a ballad known to them so well that they seemed not to listen, but simply to let the melody surge about them and provoke what thoughts it would.

At some time, perhaps many times in his life, every man is likely to meet with a thing in art or nature or human life or books which astonishes and gives him a profound satisfaction, not so much because it is rich or beautiful or strange, as because it is a symbol of a thing which, without the symbol, he could never grasp and enjoy. The German archers making a target of Leonardo's sculptured horse and horseman at Milan; the glory of purple that has flown from a painted church window and settled upon a peasant's shoulder for an hour; the eloquence of an epigram rich in anger and woe; of one bare branch that juts out from a proud green wood into the little midnight stars and makes them smaller with its splendid pang; a wood-man felling one by one the black and golden oak trees in the spring and slaying their ancient shadows; or, in a discreet and massive crowd, one jet of laughter, so full of joy or defiance or carelessness that it seems to cut through the heavy air like the whistle of a bullet – the world is one flame of these blossoms, could we but see. Music has many of them in her gift. Music, the rebel, the martyr, the victor – music, the romantic cry of matter striving to become spirit – is itself such a symbol, and there is no melody so poor that it will not at some time or another, to our watchful or receptive minds, have its festal hour in which it is crowned or at least crucified, for our solemn delight. 'Dolly Gray' I have heard sung all day by poor sluttish women as they gathered peas in the broad, burning fields of July, until it seemed that its terrible, acquiescent melancholy must have found a way to the stars and troubled them.

And of all music, the old ballads and folk songs and their airs are richest in the plain, immortal symbols. The best of them seem to be written in a language that should be universal, if only simplicity were truly simple to mankind. Their alphabet is small; their combinations are as the sunlight or the storm, and their words also are symbols. Seldom have they any direct relation to life as the realist believes it to be. They are poor in such detail as reveals a past age or a country not our own. They are in themselves epitomes of whole generations, of a whole countryside. They are the quintessence of many lives and passions made into a sweet cup for posterity. A myriad hearts and voices have in age after age poured themselves into the few notes and words. Doubtless, the old singers were not content, but we, who know them not, can well see in their old songs a kind of immortality for them in wanderings on the viewless air. The men and women – who hundreds of years ago were eating and drinking and setting their hearts on things – still retain a thin hold on life through the joy of us who hear and sing their songs, or tread their curving footpaths, or note their chisel marks on cathedral stones, or rest upon the undulating churchyard grass. The words, in league with a fair melody, lend themselves to infinite interpretations, according to the listener's heart. What great literature by known authors enables us to interpret thus by virtue of its subtlety, ballads and their music force us to do by their simplicity. The melody and the story or the song move us suddenly and launch us into an unknown. They are not art, they come to us imploring a new lease of life on the sweet earth, and so we come to give them something which the dull eye sees not in the words and notes themselves, out of our own hearts, as we do when we find a black hearthstone among the nettles, or hear the clangour of the joyous wild swan, invisible overhead, in the winter dawn.

In the parlour of the inn the singer stood up and sang of how a girl was walking alone in the meadows of spring when she saw a ship going out to sea and heard her true love crying on board; and he sailed to the wars and much he saw in strange countries, but never came back; and still she walks in the meadows and looks out to sea, though she is old, in the spring. He sang without stirring, without expression, except in so far as light and darkness from his own life emerged enmeshed among the deep notes. He might have been delivering an oracle of solemn but ambiguous things. And so in fact he was. By its simplicity and remoteness from life the song set going the potent logic of fancy which would lead many men to diverse conclusions. It excluded nothing of humanity except what baseness its melody might make impossible. The strangeness and looseness of its framework allowed each man to see himself therein, or some incident or dream in his life, or something possible to a self which he desired to be or imagined himself to be, or perhaps believed himself once to have been. There were no bounds of time or place. It included the love of Ruy Blas, of Marlowe, of Dante, of Catullus, of Kilhwch, of Swift, of Palomides, of Hazlitt, of Villon … And that little inn, in the midst of mountains and immense night, seemed a temple of all souls, where a few faithful ones still burnt candles and remembered the dead. ('The Inn', *The Heart of England*, 225–28)

Inns – Oxfordshire

Remembering this, I gave up my spiritual frivolity at Cleeve, and escaped to an inn. I suppose I had been too much taken with churchyard names in the grey evening to be quite fair to the living landlord at the inn. He was a short, heavy, fair-haired man, who had a too distinguished moustache, and talked through his nose, and had a straw hat tilted back on his neck. He and a wealthy Scotchman were talking together, and invariably – by a slight effort – agreeing with one another. His little niece came in with a flag, but he successfully put her off by saying that he had a lot of things to show her by and by, and she ran away shouting: 'Uncle has a lot of things to show me'. He explained to the Scotchman that he really had – 'flags and things for the coronation' – 'must do something' – 'every-body will' – 'have spent half a sovereign' – 'it isn't much – but still …' The child, he said, was very excitable, not that there was anything wrong; oh, no; but she would make a wonderful actress. He asked the Scotchman what he would take, and then ordered two whiskies, which I under-stood the other to pay for. They talked of drinks and of champagne, of course. The landlord began laughing at 'some *ladies*' who like it sweet. He implied huge contempt for a man who could like such stuff. Nevertheless, he hastened to say: 'You don't like sweet champagne? … No … No, of course you don't … Oh, yes, well, tastes differ'. This naturally led to Freemasonry, and it turned out that the Scotchman had done everything as a Mason (except work in stone); had served as chairman, etc. etc., and the landlord showed great eagerness of admiration by saying: 'Have you really?' several times. They returned to the subject of drink. The Scotchman announced that he took nothing but whisky, except when he had to. The landlord hastened to remark: 'You are quite right. You'll live the longer for it'. Then the landlord related how when he was three-quarters drunk he always found it so hard to drink champagne, which was only good, really, if you were run down, or for medicinal purposes. A very great deal of natural philosophy was uttered over those three or four glasses of whisky. After the Scotchman had gone the landlord was claimed by two young gentlemen who were staying under his roof for the fishing, boating, and alcoholic drinks. They called him 'Arthur,' and lured him into frivolities which he was not born to, such as arranging a band with tennis rackets, etc., for instruments, and serenading the other visitors and the inhabitants of the surrounding houses. In the intervals they fortified themselves with his whisky to such an extent that his leniency towards its effect was not to be surprised at. They also took care to keep up their reputation of commonplace luridity with the barmaid, a plain, hard-worked girl, whose smile – and, they evidently believed, everything else – was at their command. When he could slip away from these sportsmen the landlord straightened his hat and talked business to the barmaid with some anxiety and no false generosity. But they were always shouting for 'Arthur'

in shriller and more discordant voices until at last the
second fiddle of the two burst through the door of his
bedroom and rushed across and fell heavily on the other
side. Then his leader went quietly to bed. The landlord
turned to his accounts, and the barmaid went on washing
up glasses. (*The Icknield Way,* 173–75)

A Private Bar and a Tap Room – Wallingford, Oxfordshire

I crossed the bridge to the town, and went up the narrow,
old street, past an inn called 'The Shakespeare,' to the small
square of small shops, where red and blue implements
of farming stood by the pillared town hall and the sun
poured on them. I went into the 'private bar' of an inn, but
hearing only a blue-bottle and seeing little but a polished
table, and smelling nothing else, I went out and round the
comer to the taproom of the same inn. Here there were
men, politics, crops, beer, and shag tobacco.

This contrast between the 'private bar' and the taproom
round the comer reminded me of another town which
illustrates it perfectly. At the edge of the town, its large
front windows looking up the principal street, its small
back windows over a windy common to noble hills, is a
public house called 'The Jolly Drover'. The tap of 'The Jolly
Drover' is the one blot upon the face of Coldiston. The
town is clean and demure from the decent old houses of the
market-place to the brand-new cottages, more like conserv-
atories than dwellings, on the outskirts. The magistrates
are busy week after week in sentencing men and women
of all ages for begging, asking for hot water to make tea,
sleeping under hedges or in barns, for being unseemly in
act or speech; if possible, nothing offensive must happen in

the streets. A market is held once a week and is a byword in the county. Any animal can be offered for sale there; the drover creeps along behind a beast that attracts as much attention as a menagerie in the wayside villages; they know where it is going; they have seen a pig resembling a greyhound, except that it had not the strength to stand up, sold there for a shilling. Three or four times a year a builder and contractor of Coldiston is sold up, because he has been trying to get work by doing it for nothing, and these sales are the chief diversion of the neighbourhood. The town is a model of neatness and respectability, as if created by a shop-window decorator; and of all the public-houses – all named hotels – 'The Jolly Drover' is the neatest and most respectable outside, and the most expensive inside. It is painted white at short intervals. The chief barmaid is a Londoner, white-faced and coral-lipped, with a love-lock over her marble brow; and her way is brisk and knowing, and her speech more than equal to the demands made upon it of an evening by the tradesmen who will come until they are rich enough to quit the town for ever. Every form of invitation adorns the exterior.

But round the corner, towards the common, 'The Jolly Drover' is white no longer. It has no pavement outside, but a space of bare earth over-shadowed by an enormous elm's last two living branches and roughened by its wide-spreading roots. There is no invitation to enter here, but simply the words upon a low lamp, 'The Jolly Drover Tap.' No invitation is needed, for the windows are not curtained and the passer-by cannot fail to see the contented backs of drinkers and the long tiers of bottles. At night almost as much can be seen through the yellow blinds. The door stands open opposite the old tree, and through it the eye finds the bar, the plain country barmaid, the lamp, and the bright bottles. A mongrel dog or two and a gypsy's broken-down cart and wild-eyed horse are usually outside, or a tramp's woman waiting, or a group of men talking quietly before going in or after coming out. Here 'The Jolly Drover' answers to its name. It is a hedge public house of old red brick and tiles, joined, nevertheless, to the white-fronted hotel and connected with it in the proprietor's accounts. It is noisy. They sing there. No plain man is afraid to go in who has the price of half a pint in his pocket. In the summer benches are set outside, and men can sit and see the discreet going to and fro of the town life a few yards away.

Old Jack Runaway (who will borrow sixpence and then lose half a year's custom in watercress for fear of showing his face again) has lost six heifers that he was taking to the fair over the hill, but he has a pint inside and a pint before him – the clock stands still – and as the people go by he comments to himself: –

'My young Lord Drapery, may he go to gaol for being a poor beggar before he's forty. A brood mare; what with living between a policeman and a postman, with a registrar in front and a minister behind, *her* children ought to be tin soldiers. Now I wonder what's *he* worth? But if I was coined into golden sovereigns I wouldn't have married his missus when I was twenty, no, I wouldn't. Pretty Miss Ladybird, Ladybird, Ladybird, fly away from home; you're a tantalizer for a fine day, to be out with a young chap drinking a glass of six and nobody looking. What we do lose by being old, to be sure, more than by being poor! What a clean, white beard, now, that Mr. Welcome has got, like an angel. Eh, old Colonel High and Mighty, there's doctors for sciatica and gout, but there's something we have both got by being sixty that they won't cure, not if your purse is as long as your two legs. How much do *you* weigh, bombarrel? They don't allow a carriage and pair in Kingdom Come. Now, *that* young fellow could break a good few stones on a summer's day; kind, too, and don't his heels kick the pavement proud; but mind the women don't bend your back for you, or you might as well be dust to dust any day. That's what I call a good piece, neat and not too stuck up, not so young as she was, keeps the house tidy, and knows where they sell the best things cheap; now, I'd like to walk into your parlour and have a cup of tea, missus, after wiping my feet on the mat and hanging up my hat; and then that little ladybird of a nursemaid brings in the baby, and we feed it on cake and weak tea; it must be weak, or it's bad for the health ... ; and wouldn't I be proud to have you brushing my coat as I goes out of a morning, a black coat, and putting a rose in my button-hole, and kissing me before all the street – ha, ha! dirty Jack Runaway. How they do dress up the youngsters these days, like little angels; hark at them talking, and when the mother whispers to them and they run over as if you dropped it and give you a penny, you might think it would turn into a flower in their hands, and they give you a kind of look as much as to say, "God is feeding His sparrows," and then they run away without a word, and you look at the price of half a pint, and either you bless them or else you curse them. *You*, Reverend Sir, would give me a cold in the head if you were to talk; then you'd give me six-pence; if you go to heaven, there's a bit of luck left for those who don't, you freezing point, you Monday's loaf, you black-and-white undertaker's friend. Oh, this town! it's rotten without stinking, gilt without gingerbread. Look at them staring at us as if we were wild beasts taking an airing *outside* the cage ...'

The town in its turn does watch 'The Jolly Drover

Tap' and its life. Why should there be all that space wasted where the elm stands? people wonder; it is quite old-fashioned, and they smile pityingly, yet tenderly, when the old tree is crowding into leaf. But when there are half a dozen rough men and women talking aloud and gesticulating like foreigners over the price of a long, brown dog that shivers under a cart, they do not see why it should be so; only, it is 'The Jolly Drover,' and rather difficult to attack. It is extraordinary, they think as they pass by the turning down to the Tap, how a lot of lazy fellows, with nothing to do and with only rags on them, can get enough to spend half a day there. That ought certainly not to be allowed. These are not the honest poor. Either a man must work, or be looking out for work in a serious manner, or be so well dressed that he obviously need not work; or something is wrong. Nor do they invariably look starved and miserable. They eat and drink and talk to one another. Where do they come from? Of course they do not live in Coldiston: then why come here to drink? They cannot, of course, be stuffed into prison or workhouse or asylum; but is there no other cesspool possible in an age with a genius for sanitation? [...] (*The Icknield Way*, 206–13)

Inns and Books

[A]n inn should be a place where we find what we have ceased to expect at home, and not a mere 'home from home' as I have seen it modestly advertised.

An impulse as sick and as profound as the *fatigue du nord*, or as that which drove Richard Jefferies from inland meadows to the sea, goads some of us to the life of inns. Something, we may think, that overpowers the delicious sense of home, bids us exchange that for an abode that is a truer symbol of our inconstant lodging on the earth. There we are independent of every one save the boots. We can obey or ignore a distant summons easily. Perhaps even the last summons would not sound so shrill. (*Horae Solitariae*, 39)

Sleep – 'Kubla Khan'

On a walk with Wordsworth and Dorothy to Watchet and Linton 'The Ancient Mariner' was begun in November, 1797. It was finished, as Dorothy's journal says, in March, 1798. The entries relating to 'the one red leaf, the last of its clan,' etc., are supposed to 'show, not only how much Coleridge was aided by her keen observation of Nature, but fix unmistakably the date of composition of Part I' of 'Christabel'.[40] The May of 1798 was probably the month of 'Kubla Khan'. Coleridge had retired to a lonely farmhouse between Porlock and Linton. He fell asleep under the influence of opium while reading in Purchas[41] the sentence, 'Here the Khan Kubla commanded a palace to be built, and a stately garden thereunto, and thus ten miles of fertile ground were enclosed with a wall'. The poem was composed during the sleep, and would not, said Coleridge, have been so short and a fragment had not 'a person on business from Porlock' interrupted him. The 'deep romantic chasm which slanted down the green hill' alone connects it, and that tenuously, with Somerset. (*A Literary Pilgrim in England*, 184–85)

The Black Eagle and the Golden Eagle

So I came into a valley, and there was one white house in it, with a green, glowing, and humming garden, and at the door a woman who might have been the Old Year. It was one of those white houses so fair that in the old time a poet compared a girl's complexion with them, as with lilies and foam. It held all the sun, so that suddenly I knew that in another valley, farther south and further east, the rooks were making the lanes sleepy with their busy talk; the kingfishers were in pairs on the brooks, whose gentle water was waving and combing the hair of the river moss; the gold of the willow catkin was darkened by bees; over an old root of dock was a heaving colony of gleaming ants; perhaps the chiffchaff had come to the larches and the little green moschatel was in flower with large primroses among the ash stoles in wet woods; and in the splendid moments of the day the poplars seemed to come into the world, suddenly, all purple …

Yet here there was no rich high-hedged lane, no poplar, no noise of rooks, but only a desolate brown moorland crossed by deep swift brooks through which the one foot-path ran, and this white house, like a flower on a grave, recalling these memories of other valleys; so that I forgot that near by the birches stood each in a basin of foam from the dripping of mist and rain, and that I had not yet seen a thrush's nest in any hawthorn on those hills. Therefore, I counted that house as lucky for me as the Welshman's hazel-stick in the tale that is told in Iolo Morganwg's life.

This is the tale.

A Welshman, with a fine hazel-stick in his hand, was once stopped on London Bridge by an Englishman, who asked whence he came. 'From my own country,' said the Welshman churlishly. 'Do not take it amiss,' said the Englishman; 'and if you will tell me what I ask, and take my advice, it will be much for your good. Under the roots of the tree from which came your stick, there are great treasures of gold and silver; if you can remember the place, and will take me to it, I will make the treasure yours.'

Now knowing that the fellow was a magician, the Welshman, though at first unwilling to be a party in this strange thing, at length agreed, and went with him to Craig-y-Dinas and showed him the hazel-tree. They dug out the root and found a broad flat stone underneath, which covered the entrance to a cave. They went in, the magician warning the Welshman lest he should touch a bell that hung in the middle of their path. At the spacious further end of the cave, they saw many warriors lying asleep in a circle, with bright armour on, and weapons ready at hand. One of the warriors, refulgent above all the rest, had a jewelled and golden crown along with the shield and battle-axe at his side.

At the feet of the warriors, in the middle of the circle, they saw two immense heaps, the one of gold, the other of silver, and the magician told the Welshman that he might take away as much as he could carry from either of the heaps. So he took much gold. The magician took nothing. On their way out of the cave he again warned the Welshman lest he should touch the bell. But should he touch it, said the magician, some of the warriors would surely awake and ask 'if it was yet day': to which he must at once answer: 'No, sleep thou on,' whereupon the warriors would sleep again. And this the Welshman found to be truth when he staggered under his gold and grazed the bell; but remembering the other's words, he said: 'Sleep thou on' when the warriors asked if it were day; and they slept.

When they had left the cave, and closed the entrance, the magician told the Welshman that he might return to the cave whenever he wished; that the warriors were the knights of King Arthur, and the warrior with the jewelled and golden crown was King Arthur; that they were awaiting the day when the Black Eagle and the Golden Eagle should go to war; for on that day the trembling earth would toll the bell, and at that sound the king and the knights of the king would awake, take their weapons, overthrow the Saxon, recover the island of Britain, and again establish their king at Caerlleon, in justice and in peace and for ever. But the Welshman spent his gold. He went again to the cave; he overloaded his back with gold; he stumbled and the bell rang; he forgot the password. And the knights rose and leaned upon their elbows, and one of them stood up and took away his gold and beat him and thrust him out and closed the mouth of the cave; and though he and many others made all the hill sore with their digging, the cave was not found again. (*Beautiful Wales*, 121–25)

'The Trumpet' (September 1916, *Poems*)

> Rise up, rise up,
> And, as the trumpet blowing
> Chases the dreams of men,
> As the dawn glowing
> The stars that left unlit
> The land and water,
> Rise up and scatter
> The dew that covers
> The print of last night's lovers –
> Scatter it, scatter it!

While you are listening
To the clear horn,
Forget, men, everything
On this earth newborn,
Except that it is lovelier
Than any mysteries.
Open your eyes to the air
That has washed the eyes of the stars
Through all the dewy night:
Up with the light,
To the old wars;
Arise, arise!

Night Sounds

I lay awake for some time listening to the motor-cars. Most of them rushed through the town; a few came there to rest and silence; others paused for a minute only with drumming suspense. I thought I should not easily tire of these signals from unknown travellers. Not that I spent much time on definite and persistent conjecture as to who they were, whence they had come, and whither and why they travelled. I was too sleepy, though at any time such a labour would have been irksome. No; I was more than content to let these noises compose a wordless music of mystery and adventure within my brain. The cars could bring together lovers or enemies or conspirators so swiftly that their mid-night alarums suggest nothing else. It is hard to connect their subjugated frenzy with mere stupid haste. The little light steals through a darkness so vast that the difference between a star and a lantern is nothing to it. The thing is so suitable for a great adventure that straightway the mind conceives one. Hark! on a winter's night the

sound and the idea are worthy of the storm and in harmony
with it: –

> Hark 'tis an elfin storm from fairyland,
> Of haggard seeming but a boon indeed[42] ...

It was easy to imagine myself the partner in magnificent
risks quite outside my own experience, and to feel the
glory and even the danger with no touch of pain, whilst I
lay as careless as the friendly near neighbourhood of sleep
could make me. The touch of arrogance in the voice of
the motor is to its credit by night. In a measure it revives
the romantic and accepted arrogance of horn and trumpet.
It gives at least an outward bravery which has long been
dropping away from drivers of horses. I do not disparage
the sound of hoofs and wheels and the private voice of a
solitary traveller on the dark roads, but there is something
melancholy in it, and more endurance than enterprise ...
But, above all, the sounds of the motor-car have added
immensely to the London night, at least for good sleepers
with minds at ease. Formerly, to those out of the Covent
Garden routes, the only sound of night travel at all
provoking to the mind was the after-midnight hansom's
clatter, which challenged conjecture more often than
imagination; I pictured most likely a man with bleared eyes
and a white shirt who had let his cigar out – at most, a
man whose achievement was behind rather than before
him; and certainly I was always very well content to be in
bed. But the motor-horn is turbulent and daring, though it
may be innocent to say so. Even if it is coming home there
is a proud possibility of distance left behind, and either it
seems that the arrivers have not returned for nothing or the
sudden stop suggests at the least a sublimity of dejection
from proud heights. As to the car setting out in darkness,

it gathers to itself all the pomp of setting out, as we have imagined or read of it in stories of soldiers, travellers or lovers, and as we have experienced it when children, going to fish or to find bird's nests or mushrooms, and as we still fancy it would be for ourselves, were we ever to advance towards adventures. I suppose, also, that the speed of a motor-car, to the outsider, unconsciously suggests a race, an unknown, end, an untold prize … These thoughts and mere listening to the horns and machinery occupied me and led on to sleep in such a manner that I ignored a man next door imitating a gramophone quite seriously, and in less than half an hour I was asleep and began to dream drivel. (*Icknield Way*, 100–03)

'A Dream' (July 1915, *Last Poems*)

Over known fields with an old friend in dream
I walked, but came sudden to a strange stream.
Its dark waters were bursting out most bright
From a great mountain's heart into the light.
They ran a short course under the sun, then back
Into a pit they plunged, once more as black
As at their birth; and I stood thinking there
How white, had the day shone on them, they were,
Heaving and coiling. So by the roar and hiss
And by the mighty motion of the abyss
I was bemused, that I forgot my friend
And neither saw nor sought him till the end,
When I awoke from waters unto men
Saying: 'I shall be here some day again.'

An Autumn House

Because sleep clothes the feet of sorrow with leaden sandals and fastens eagles' wings upon the heels of joy, I wonder that some ask at nightfall what the morrow shall see concluded: I would rather ask what sleep shall bring forth, and whither I shall travel in my dreams. It seems indeed to me that to sleep is owed a portion of the deliberation given to death. If life is an apprenticeship to death, waking may be an education for sleep. We are not thoughtful enough about sleep; yet it is more than half of that great portion of life spent really in solitude. 'Nous sommes tous dans le desert! Personne ne comprend personne.'[43] In the desert what then shall we do? We truly ought to enter upon sleep as into a strange, fair chapel. Fragrant and melodious ante-chamber of the unseen, sleep is a novitiate for the beyond. Nevertheless, it is likely that those who compose themselves carefully for sleep are few as those who die holily; and most are ignorant of an art of sleeping (as of dying). The surmises, the ticking of the heart, of an anxious child, – the awful expectation of Columbus spying the fringes of a world, – such are my emotions, as I go to rest. I know not whether before the morrow I shall not pass by the stars of heaven and behold the 'pale chambers of the west,' returning before dawn. To many something like Jacob's dream often happens. The angels rising are the souls of the dreamers dignified by the insignia of sleep. Without vanity, I think in my boyhood, in my sleep, I was often in heaven. Since then, I have gone dreaming by another path, and heard the sighs and chatterings of the underworld; have gone from my pleasant bed to a fearful neighbourhood, like the fifth Emperor Henry [1081–

1125], who, for penance, when lights were out, the watch fast asleep, walked abroad barefoot, leaving his imperial habiliments, leaving Matilda the Empress. And when the world is too much with me, when the past is a reproach harrying me with dreadful faces, the present a fierce mockery, the future an open grave, it is sweet to sleep. I have closed a well-loved book, ere the candle began to fail, that I might sleep, and let the soul take her pleasure in the deeps of eternity. It may be that the light of morning is ever cold, when it breaks in upon my sleep and disarrays the palaces of my dreams. (Extract from 'An Autumn House', *Rose Acre Papers*, 105–07)

NOTES AND REFERENCES

40 Edward Thomas refers to *Samuel Taylor Coleridge: A Narrative of the Events of his Life,* by James Dykes Campbell (London: Macmillan, 1894).

41 *Purchas: his Pilgrimage; or Relations of the World and Religions Observed in All Ages and Places Discovered, from the Creation to the Present,* by Samuel Purchas, 1613.

42 This is a quote from John Keat's poem 'The Eve of St. Agnes' (from 1820) – though the punctuation is unusual.

43 Gustave Flaubert, correspondence.

Chapter Ten

Folk Traditions

Thomas's story about Llewellyn the Bard from *Beautiful Wales* is fictitious, and the poem he included in this section as a 'translation' is actually Thomas's first published poem (see his letter to Gordon Bottomley, 30 June 1905), here described as an 'imitative song'. Thomas knew several Welsh writers well – including the real-life Bard John Jenkins, or Gwili, from Carmarthenshire, and Owen M. Edwards, from Bala, who was his tutor at Oxford and an advocate of literature in the Welsh language.

Earlier, we saw that Thomas based early poems on folk weather rhymes, and wrote stories for old proverbs. His poem 'Lob' is based on his many encounters with real and fictitious countryman (like 'Jack-Runaway, in the previous chapter), and a variety of Puckish country characters from folklore. Rather than denigrating his 'Lob' as a redneck or a 'hick', Thomas gave Lob magical powers like Shakespeare's Puck, who was a hobgoblin (or a 'hob'), and emphasised the countryman's knowledge of things that matter, such as the names of plants: 'in a tender mood he, as I guess, / Christened one flower Love-in-idleness, /And while he walked from Exeter to Leeds /One April called all cuckoo-flowers Milkmaids'.

Although Thomas's interest in oral traditions started in childhood with the legends of Wales and Arthur, it was aided by the long 19th century Folk Revival championed, amongst others, by Cecil Sharp and harnessed by Thomas in *The Pocket Book of Poems and Songs for the Open Air* (1907). *The Heart of England* included songs first transcribed by George Rathbone from the Westmoreland Music Festival. Thomas's two poems named 'An Old Song' were based on his favourite English folk songs, 'The Lincolnshire Poacher' (which also appears in *The Pocket Book* and his anthology *This England*) and 'A Rovin'. He endowed them with personal symbolism and meaning, including his interest in trespassing. Like footpaths and old roads, Thomas thought that folk songs and stories allowed us to give life to the past. However, Thomas was not limited to English traditions – he also collected stories from Wales and Ireland, and Norse tales.

In *The South Country* he asked, '[c]an [ballads] possibly give a vigorous impulse to a new school of poetry that shall treat the life of our time and what in the past has most meaning for us as freshly as those ballads did the life of their times?' (1909: 58). Thomas showed in his own poetry that they could.

Tales – Cwellyn Lake

And there is Severn in its wild and unnoted childhood, its lovely and gallant youth, its noble and romantic prime, as it leaves Wales and passes Shrewsbury, the pattern of all famous streams –
Fluminaque antiques subterlabentia muros;[44]
and its solemn, grey, and mighty and worldly-wise old age, listening to its latest daughter the Wye,
where it has a cry from the sea, a cry from the
mountain;[45]
and Clwyd and Conway and Ceiriog and Aled and Dovey, streams that remember princes and bards; and the little waters flowing from Cwellyn Lake, of which a story is told.

Near the river which falls from Cwellyn Lake, they say that the fairies used to dance in a meadow on fair moonlit nights. One evening the heir to the farm of Ystrad, to which the meadow belonged, hid himself in a thicket near the meadow. And while the fairies were dancing, he ran out and carried off one of the fairy women. The others at once disappeared. She resisted and cried, but he led her to his home, where he was tender to her, so that she was willing to remain as his maid-servant. But she would not tell him her name. Some time afterward he again saw the fairies in the meadow and overheard one of them saying, 'The last time we met here, our sister Penelope was snatched away from us by one of the mortals'. So he returned and offered to marry her, because she was hard-working and beautiful. For a long time she would not consent; but at last she gave way, on the condition 'that if ever he should strike her with iron, she would leave him and never return to him again'. They were happy together for many years; and she bore him a son and a daughter; and so wise and active was she, that he became one of the richest men of that country, and besides the farm of Ystrad, he farmed all the lands on the north side of Nant-y-Bettws to the top of Snowdon, and all Cwm Brwynog in Llanberis, or about five thousand acres. But one day Penelope went with him into a field to catch a horse; and as the horse ran away from him, he was angry and threw the bridle at him, but struck Penelope instead. She disappeared. He never saw her again, but one night afterward he heard her voice at his window, asking him to take care of the children, in these words:

Oh, lest my son should suffer cold,
Him in his father's coat enfold:
Lest cold should seize my darling fair,
For her, her mother's robe prepare.

These children and their descendants were called the *Pellings*, says the teller of the tale; and 'there are,' he adds, 'still living several opulent and respectable persons who are known to have sprung from the Pellings. The best blood in my own veins is this fairy's.'[46] (*Beautiful Wales*, 18–20)

Llewelyn the Bard

Of Llewelyn, the bard, I cannot decide whether he most loves man or men. He is for ever building castles in the air and filling them with splendid creatures, whom he calls men. Then he laments that he cannot find any like them on hill or in valley: when, straightway, he will meet some human being, old friend or passing stranger, on the road or in a shop, and away go the phantoms of his castles, and he is wild in adoration of the new thing he has found. His grandmother, by the way, was called a fairy's child, though the truth seems to have been that her mother was a gipsy girl. Perhaps that is why he has no creed but many creeds, and was looked upon with great favour by the Calvinists until they found that he liked the Church as well. Yet I think that he likes men truly because they remind him of something he has read or dreamed, or because they make him dream; herein somewhat resembling the fellow who paid much court to another because he reminded him of the late Duke of –, and he was a lover of dukes. Or he is like some that have seen processions of phantoms and say that sometimes the phantoms are simply fairies speaking an unknown tongue, but that sometimes several have the faces and voices of some among the dead whom they used to know. Why he is so glad to be among us at the farmhouse

I have not discovered, but I suppose we remind him of Hebrew prophets or Greekish kings, for of our established merits he takes no thought.

I think he wastes so much pity for Annie of Lochroyan that other maids find him passionless, and he grows tender over Burd Ellen and Cynisca as their lovers never did. Arthur and Gwalchmai and Gwenhwyvar, the most unreal and unliving of all the persons of literature, please him most. In a world where all things are passing, he loves best those things which, having past and having left a ghost of fame behind, can live for ever in minds like his. In London he saw but a place where marsh and river and woods had been and might be again; or where

> Sometimes a lily petal floated down
> From dear, remote pools to the dreary town;

where the gulls flew over in the mournful January light; where a few friends had fires and lamps and books – their light faintly flickering in tremendous gloom and making one faint reality in the place; where wind and rain some-times brought the past again; for the very touch of rain and wind beckoned to him, as it is fabled that the foam driven from waters that cover old towns will draw the unwary whom it touches into the deeps.

He himself professes to care only for his own childhood and youth; only he is aware, as not every one is, that the childhood began in Eden, and is ages old, so that, after all, the few years that make middle age do not count for much. His life and his way of looking at it remind me of a story of a young Eastern prince. Every day, from his early childhood, a story-teller had told him a tale. But, soon after he was sixteen, the story-teller came to him, and, falling on his knees, told him that he had no more stories to tell.

The young prince fell into a rage and swore that he would kill the man if, in a week, he had no new story ready. And the story-teller, who was very old and unwilling to die, went into the desert and neither ate nor drank, and made a plan by which to save his life. So he returned to the young prince, who asked if he had a new story, and he said that he had. And the prince bade him tell the story; and he began to speak, and told the prince the story which he had told him first, when he was a small child; and the prince was pleased. And until the old man died, he never told a story which he had not told before; and the prince was always pleased.

His poetry, if it could be understood, might be counted great, and perhaps it is so in a world where trees and animals are reverenced in a way which is hardly dawning here. He is a kind of mad Blake. He sees the world from among the stars, and those who see it from an elevation of five or six feet, and think that they see it as it really is, are not satisfied. He would make human the stars and seasons; he would make starry the flowers and the grass. He would have it that the world is but a shadow of Blake's 'Real and Eternal world':[47] that we who are shadows cling to the superstition that we are not, and have but prejudiced and fearful ears for his prophecies. He sees the world as a commonwealth of angels and men and beasts and herbs; and in it, horrible discords that we others scarcely hear seem to him to strike the stars.

[...]

And here is one of his imitative songs, reduced to its lowest terms by a translator:

> She is dead, Eluned,
> Whom the young men and the old men
> And the old women and even the young women

Came to the gates in the village
To see, because she walked as beautifully as a heifer.

She is dead, Eluned,
Who sang the new songs
And the old; and made the new
Seem old, and the old
As if they were just born and she had christened
them.

She is dead, Eluned,
Whom I admired and loved,
When she was gathering red apples,
When she was making bread and cakes,
When she was smiling to herself alone and not
thinking of me.

She is dead, Eluned,
Who was part of Spring,
And of blue Summer and red Autumn,
And made the Winter beloved;
She is dead, and these things come not again.

(Beautiful Wales, 77–83)

The Origins of Celtic Folk Tales

These tales are founded upon ancient ones, the work of
Welshmen and Irishmen when Wales and Ireland were
entirely independent of England. The Welsh tales come
from a book now known as the *Mabinogion*. They were
written down at the end of the Middle Ages, and translated
from Welsh into English by Lady Guest in the nineteenth
century. The original Welsh manuscript (called *The Red
Book of Hergest*, because it was once at Hergest in Radnor)

belongs to the fourteenth and fifteenth centuries, but the stories had been told over and over again, and probably written down many times, before they were copied into *The Red Book*. They were being told in the years between the Norman conquest of England and Edward I's conquest of Wales. But the subjects of them were much earlier. Even those who told the tales would, perhaps, have been unable to say when a man as huge as Bran was ruling at Harlech, nor did they consider the matter any more than children today consider the tale of 'Jack the Giant-killer' in its relation to scientific fact. But in 'Kilhugh and Olwen' and ' The Dream of Rhonabwy' King Arthur appears. The men who told these two stories were probably thinking of a glorious heroic age, when Arthur was a supreme king, resisting the Roman and Saxon invader. They gave a strange reality to some of the wonders by connecting them with actual places in Wales, so that a man today could walk in the steps of Kilhugh and Rhonabwy. Even 'The Dream of Maxen', which is about a Roman emperor, comes to its height and to its end in Wales, and in places which are still to be seen. Very little was known to the mediaeval writers about the age of the Saxon invaders and the seventh-century King Arthur, except that it was one of greater men than any that were living; and therefore they described their heroes as if they were Welsh and Norman warriors in dress and manners, but of greater stature and prowess. They were certain that Arthur had once been king in Britain, and they were ready to come to blows with men who denied it [...]

So in Ireland, the tale of Deirdre was one which the poets had to know, and the Irish told their tales over and over again, age after age, adding to them and taking away, as the Welsh did. They were still more clear about their heroes, though the stories as we have them are very little earlier than the Welsh, and were therefore written down long after the events were supposed to have taken place. Consequently, the kind of life described, when it is not in our eyes impossible, is the life of the storyteller's own age in Christian Ireland. As in 'Kilhugh', so in one of the Irish tales, 'There is scarcely a hill, valley, river, rock, mound, or cave in the line of country from Emania in the present county of Armagh to Lusk in that of Dublin, of which the ancient and often varying names and history are not to be found' in it.[48] (extract from 'Note on Sources', *Celtic Stories*, 126–27)

'Lob' (April 1915, *Poems*)

> At hawthorn-time in Wiltshire travelling
> In search of something chance would never bring,
> An old man's face, by life and weather cut
> And coloured, – rough, brown, sweet as any
>   nut, –
> A land face, sea-blue-eyed, – hung in my mind
> When I had left him many a mile behind.
> All he said was: 'Nobody can't stop 'ee'. It's
> A footpath, right enough. You see those bits
> Of mounds – that's where they opened up the
>   barrows
> Sixty years since, while I was scaring sparrows.
> They thought as there was something to find there,
> But couldn't find it, by digging, anywhere.'
>
> To turn back then and seek him, where was the use?
> There were three Manningfords, – Abbots, Bohun,
>   and Bruce:
> And whether Alton, not Manningford, it was,
> My memory could not decide, because

There was both Alton Barnes and Alton Priors.
All had their churches, graveyards, farms, and byres,
Lurking to one side up the paths and lanes,
Seldom well seen except by aeroplanes;
And when bells rang, or pigs squealed, or cocks
        crowed,
Then only heard. Ages ago the road
Approached. The people stood and looked and
        turned,
Nor asked it to come nearer, nor yet learned
To move out there and dwell in all men's dust.
And yet withal they shot the weathercock, just
Because 'twas he crowed out of tune, they said:
So now the copper weathercock is dead.
If they had reaped their dandelions and sold
Them fairly, they could have afforded gold.

Many years passed, and I went back again
Among those villages, and looked for men
Who might have known my ancient. He himself
Had long been dead or laid upon the shelf,
I thought. One man I asked about him roared
At my description: ''Tis old Bottlesford
He means, Bill.' But another said: 'Of course,
It was Jack Button up at the White Horse.
He's dead, sir, these three years.' This lasted till
A girl proposed Walker of Walker's Hill,
'Old Adam Walker. Adam's Point you'll see
Marked on the maps.'

            'That was her roguery,'
The next man said. He was a squire's son
Who loved wild bird and beast, and dog and gun
For killing them. He had loved them from his birth,
One with another, as he loved the earth.

'The man may be like Button, or Walker, or
Like Bottlesford, that you want, but far more
He sounds like one I saw when I was a child.
I could almost swear to him. The man was wild
And wandered. His home was where he was free.
Everybody has met one such man as he.
Does he keep clear old paths that no one uses
But once a life-time when he loves or muses?
He is English as this gate, these flowers, this mire.
And when at eight years old Lob-lie-by-the-fire
Came in my books, this was the man I saw.
He has been in England as long as dove and daw,
Calling the wild cherry tree the merry tree,
The rose campion Bridget-in-her-bravery;
And in a tender mood he, as I guess,
Christened one flower Love-in-idleness,
And while he walked from Exeter to Leeds
One April called all cuckoo-flowers Milkmaids.
From him old herbal Gerard learnt, as a boy,
To name wild clematis the Traveller's-joy.
Our blackbirds sang no English till his ear
Told him they called his Jan Toy "Pretty dear."
(She was Jan Toy the Lucky, who, having lost
A shilling, and found a penny loaf, rejoiced.)
For reasons of his own to him the wren
Is Jenny Pooter. Before all other men
'Twas he first called the Hog's Back the Hog's
    Back.
That Mother Dunch's Buttocks should not lack
Their name was his care. He too could explain
Totteridge and Totterdown and Juggler's Lane:
He knows, if anyone. Why Tumbling Bay,
Inland in Kent, is called so, he might say.

'But little he says compared with what he does.
If ever a sage troubles him he will buzz
Like a beehive to conclude the tedious fray:
And the sage, who knows all languages, runs away.
Yet Lob has thirteen hundred names for a fool,
And though he never could spare time for school
To unteach what the fox so well expressed,
On biting the cock's head off, – Quietness is best, –
He can talk quite as well as anyone
After his thinking is forgot and done.
He first of all told someone else's wife,
For a farthing she'd skin a flint and spoil a knife
Worth sixpence skinning it. She heard him speak:
"She had a face as long as a wet week"
Said he, telling the tale in after years.
With blue smock and with gold rings in his ears,
Sometimes he is a pedlar, not too poor
To keep his wit. This is tall Tom that bore
The logs in, and with Shakespeare in the hall
Once talked, when icicles hung by the wall.
As Herne the Hunter he has known hard times.
On sleepless nights he made up weather rhymes
Which others spoilt. And, Hob being then his name,
He kept the hog that thought the butcher came
To bring his breakfast "You thought wrong," said
    Hob.
When there were kings in Kent this very Lob,
Whose sheep grew fat and he himself grew merry,
Wedded the king's daughter of Canterbury;
For he alone, unlike squire, lord, and king,
Watched a night by her without slumbering;
He kept both waking. When he was but a lad
He won a rich man's heiress, deaf, dumb, and sad,
By rousing her to laugh at him. He carried

His donkey on his back. So they were married.
And while he was a little cobbler's boy
He tricked the giant coming to destroy
Shrewsbury by flood. "And how far is it yet?"
The giant asked in passing. "I forget;
But see these shoes I've worn out on the road
And we're not there yet." He emptied out his load
Of shoes for mending. The giant let fall from his
    spade
The earth for damming Severn, and thus made
The Wrekin hill; and little Ercall hill
Rose where the giant scraped his boots. While still
So young, our Jack was chief of Gotham's sages.
But long before he could have been wise, ages
Earlier than this, while he grew thick and strong
And ate his bacon, or, at times, sang a song
And merely smelt it, as Jack the giant-killer
He made a name. He too ground up the miller,
The Yorkshireman who ground men's bones for
    flour.

'Do you believe Jack dead before his hour?
Or that his name is Walker, or Bottlesford,
Or Button, a mere clown, or squire, or lord?
The man you saw, – Lob-lie-by-the-fire, Jack Cade,
Jack Smith, Jack Moon, poor Jack of every trade,
Young Jack, or old Jack, or Jack What-d'ye-call,
Jack-in-the-hedge, or Robin-run-by-the-wall,
Robin Hood, Ragged Robin, lazy Bob,
One of the lords of No Man's Land, good Lob, –
Although he was seen dying at Waterloo,
Hastings, Agincourt, and Sedgemoor too, –
Lives yet. He never will admit he is dead
Till millers cease to grind men's bones for bread,
Not till our weathercock crows once again

And I remove my house out of the lane
On to the road.' With this he disappeared
In hazel and thorn tangled with old-man's-beard.
But one glimpse of his back, as there he stood,
Choosing his way, proved him of old Jack's blood
Young Jack perhaps, and now a Wiltshireman
As he has oft been since his days began.

The Passing of Pan

Amidst a wood I came once upon an idiot, seated on a fallen tree, and was astonished by the classic beauty of his posture and the curls of golden hair on his head. His lips were empurpled by wild fruit. Just one bead of blood adhered to his singularly clear cheeks. The face was noble; only the mouth was discordant – rather large, and like a child's, uncontrolled. He must have been godlike as a child. Now, all but this had grown up and left the eyes wandering and the mouth lisping in a disappointing way. Fresh and bright as the fur of a beast, his long hair was full of dead leaves, with one crow's feather. His lips continually wavered with murmuring sounds. His dress I did not observe, because, I suppose, it became him naturally, after the manner of all the poor. As I went by he plucked and gave me a reed. He meant to give me one with a flower, and did not see his mistake, I thought. The look of expectancy, as of a brute for food, confused me, so that he laughed, showing his red tongue between his white teeth. Before leaving, I gave him a coin, which he scornfully cast away and continued his murmuring. But I had not gone far when I heard him ferreting about in the underwood where it fell. He was searching for it doubtless, while his cry, soon after, a very melodious one, was full of triumph at the find. I had, however, nearly forgotten him, the hour verging on sunset and unfavourable to the recollection of such matters, when he came up rapidly and grunting aloud, though in perfect composure like a beast out of breath, to offer me a little sheaf of fragrant reeds, all flowerless as before. He laid the weight of his hand on my shoulder and watched my lips as I spoke, imitating them with his own, breathing all the time lustily into my face. With what surprise I noticed the savage but not unclean flavour of his breath and the indefinable scent of grass, herbs and bark! With a repetition of his melodious cry and a petulant stamp he went away into the wood. Afterwards I learnt that he hoarded coin for the purchase of honey, in quest of which he was irresistible. By this food he was easily intoxicated. The half malign juices of the forest combined in the honey to overthrow the feeble brain, for Nature has odd, immoderate ways of putting into action her empire over men. For the rest, I was able to learn much of the idiot's way. He would often sit motionless for hours in the great wood, looking at naught, while the birds used rude, pretty intimacies towards him. Children had seen him listening for a voice at the trunk of an oak tree on moody summer days. Once he had been detected in a four-footed pursuit of rabbits by means of a keen, and (as it were) reasoning sense of smell.

Years afterwards I came again. But he was painfully changed. He was tending several fat horses tethered in a lane of hawthorn and waving wild hops, where the country people sauntered by to church, gaily apparelled in purple and crimson, so as to check one's breathing on that fiery day; the neat wives bounded alongside their ungainly husbands, so light and graceful as to seem merely the clouds scattered by them in their walk. Now and then the children teased him. He recognised me at once, laying his hand tentatively on my shoulder, with the words, 'I am very cold!' My teeth chattered at the touch. Being in haste, I gave him tobacco and passed onward.

Next morning I met a strolling piper at the inn, who was full of stories about his masterful pipe. In one place he had piped a city street silent, then into a dance; in another, a fellow had split his instrument that he might find the secret – a smell of tobacco smoke apparently. 'But the greatest fun was late last night.' He had been journeying towards the inn, piping a melody he had learned in Wales, when he heard footsteps following. He piped on. The steps reeled; it must have been a drunkard. Still he pursued, through pond and copse, until he dropped, probably in cosy grasses, out in the moonlight. 'But he must have risen long ago to escape the lightning and rain.'

I hurried out in alarm. It must be the idiot! I said: Heaven knows how the night would deal with him.

At a distance I recognised my friend, as he lay in the short grass, with rooks feeding many yards clear of him. His loose mouth was evenly shut. His chin closed the lines of his face very handsomely with an emphasis unlike its wont, through the clinging wet beard. The rain had left his face white and polished, except where friendly small birds had been tapping the corners of his eyes, with intent to awaken him. A shower of petals had not yet shrivelled on his breast, and gave a fresh smell in the rainy air; the two stately horses forgot to graze where they stood. In fact, he was dead, a clay pipe rigid between his teeth.

While I stood there, pondering the wonderful beauty of the corpse, which seemed now to be enjoying a perfect kind of life, perfect calm, certainly to be far more impressive than the moving frame, and to have gotten all that was once lacking, the piper came up. Perhaps his were the sensations of the hunter who has struck down some lovely harmless bird; at least he was deeply moved. For he understood the whole event immediately, and readily showed when I asked for the instrument that he had been playing on the last night. To my surprise he drew from his pocket a simple set of reeds bound side by side together. They reminded me of the reeds I had been given so strangely in the wood long ago; and to my inquiry how he had come by this peculiar kind, for the thing was evidently his own handiwork, he answered in such a manner that I was convinced that the dead man had been the giver of the reeds. At this he was greatly distressed, and parted eagerly with the pipe at my request. The body was buried in solitude. That day I hurried westward to a distant town.

The shorn wheat-fields in that mounded country were of a pale fluid yellow that mingled with the sky's blue, and was only here and there invaded by the lustrous green of an aftermath or the solid shadow of an immense elm; in it the little woods actually seemed to float. Meadowsweet like foam, and a small scabious flower always haunted by blue butterflies of the same hue, lingered by the wayside, with faint red campions and cranesbills, and yellow buttercups, hawk-weeds, ragwort, and agrimony spires. On a white cottage wall flowered several great red roses. In a hedge I found one hawkweed blossom of a deep flame colour, like a dusky volcanic fire creeping out of the stones, the colour of the sun then about to set. One or two bramble leaves had been coloured likewise, but with green veins remaining. Placid and yet luxurious, there was something in the sunset like the old age of Lucullus. The sun itself was burning mildly and warm; the dark trees towards the west lay round it like a party of children half circling a fire, and listening to strange tales.

For in September, the early evening of the year, when darkness and light, Summer and Winter, meet without contention and combine their loveliest symbols, at sunset, a profound sense of the whole past of men and Nature is born of the sense of the year that is passing and the season that is dead, and we individuals are blended with the universe in one mellow, tranquil passion of regret. Launched by this passion upon a course of many memories, I was still far from land when I fell into deep sleep; and in my sleep I had a dream.

The mind takes a delight in contrast as one refuge from the present; so in my dream it was broad noon; and because the actual season was autumn, the atmosphere of my dream was that of spring, of early spring with its poignant colours. A great forest hung round about. The might of its infinite silence and repose, indeed, never ceased to weigh upon me in my dream. I could hear sounds: they were leagues away. The trees which I could see were few: I felt that they must be thousands deep on every hand. Just where I found myself, the trees opened wide apart and enclosed a fair space of sunlight and flowery grass. At the edge of this space arborets of underwood grew, whose foliage turned to rough silver in the sun. Beyond, trees of every kind clustered together, or, rather, stood each in its own demesne, at aristocratic distance, not as in English woods. Airy, noiseless acacias were there; stilly, religious oaks; beeches, with boughs like human limbs, disclosed here and there by the light cirrus foliage, and possessed of liquid voices in their glossy, humid leaves; volatile birches; fruit trees that mounted stiffly to a certain height, where they threw off their stony character and expanded into waves of branch work and flying spray of leaves; and beneath many, the palmy hemlock climbed the air as meaner plants climb the bushes. Not one of the trees but cast an ample shadow, like the train of a mantle falling from their shoulders and spreading outward on the sward. As the day grew, the trees appeared to retreat into the wood and leave their trains upon the grass.

Suddenly out of this great silence came the figure of a youth, walking with downward eyes, placid pace, and an attitude that expressed all the flattering thoughts of happy love and joy in life. There was much harmony in the transient grouping of his limbs, as he walked – in the raised and rounded knee, in the foot balanced on the air as on a step. A profusion of hair covered his temples like a tawny fleece thrown over his head in play. Coming nearer, his face told of a passion far deeper than for any maiden, though of a maiden he thought. His skin, like rose leaves, too pure to be red, too healthy to be white, had a kind of ardency or radiance, such as is seen in women, which subtly expounds a kinship between soul and mere bodily breath that men rarely show.

After he had long been in sight, a wondrous clear music arose, the music of a human voice fluting cunningly, for now and again the voice stopped and the singer let silence speak for him in the interval; but took up the strain again, naturally as when the tones of a nightingale emerge from the quiet night, whilst the forest is listening, aware. The youth presently turned in search of this voice. In my dream I followed him.

When I saw him next, he was leaning upon a blossomy crag. The light just there was green under the trees like sunny ocean water. He was listening, eyes closed, 'all ear'. On the other side of the crag a terrible figure stood near him, unobserved.

The figure seemed to be that of Pan, changed by the long wanderings since he fled, in advance of the general banishment of the Olympians, before the westward marches of Roman legionaries. He had often gone on hands and feet. The stones had bitten his flesh. He had drunken of his own tears. This very day the clap of axes and the volleying sound of trees falling invaded his cave. The wild bees chased him away from his customary pittance of honeycomb. Thus tormented, he was first aware of his rapid undeification. While the wild creatures avoided their suspicious co-mate more than human beings, one consolation was still effective. He retained his pipe, and could play! Moreover, sorrow had sweetened his voice – that voice to which the youth was listening, not by chance, it would seem, if one might judge from Pan's anxious sentry over the forest pathways, and the persistence of his tunes. The encounter was apparently aforethought, and welcome to Pan. He was surely looking for something from this stranger that other wayfarers could not give. For the many wayfarers, threading the forest like puppet forms, with all their fatigue and ungainliness, flattered the languid self-esteem of the embittered god by comparison; so much so, that he amused himself by piping them far astray from their companions, playing upon their fears, until at last, horn and hoof under cover, in the guise of a mute rustic, he led them safely back, and disappeared without their thanks. But that was a slender triumph. Afterwards he often mused, reviewing the treasures of his memory, drawing fresh powers from silence, and compacting all into one brilliant song that took flight as if it must penetrate heaven, but falling splendidly, seemed to bury itself in earth with shrieks. He would then lament that this melody was mortal nevertheless; he had listened to men singing like that! And he was filled with a supreme pity – pity for the flowers, the grass, for all things that quickly pass away. To prove his old supremacy in music he must, then, compete with one of the loftiest among those mortals whom he so despised. With this in view, he seemed now to be in peaceable ambuscade; yet with such a rival, he would loathe to do his best.

The song he was now singing made much of reminiscences of the old time, but seemed to have been turned in such a way that it should overpower the youth by the strange fascination of the forest life, enjoyed in animal liberty and with spiritual reflection. It expressed the inexpressible magic of certain hours and places; of autumn's holy purple eve, for example; of landscapes beheld in a kind of haze of the spirit; of the moon-enriched flood, the moon aloft with all her stars. It was full of the idiom of trees and the motion of great waters.

At a pause in the song, the youth quaked to see the horned brow, the fleecy hair on the legs, and the slender bony calves ending in cloven feet, that seemed to connect the singer with the brutes, whose covering changes character in some one place at least, as at heel or muzzle, as if to remind one of the earth.

The song broke again in a fountain of clear sound from the coarse throat. One hand lay on the youth's neck, like ice; the other hung down, grasping a seven-reeded pipe, which Pan raised to his own lips in the pauses and seemed to play – but silently. Something fond crept into the expression of that touch and the anxious little eyes fixed on the youth, as though to evoke and translate his inmost thought. Pan also was leaning on the rock, but towered above the youth. For by a brute-like artifice he was hoisted up so that only the point of one foot grated the earth.

After he had again checked the melody, Pan offered the reeds to the youth, earnestly inviting him to play. But he refused. When the god insisted, he refused a second time, saying, 'Tempt me not. The limits of my being are overthrown. If I were to play, my music would be my doom.'

To which the god, in harmonious speech, made an angry reply: 'Stupid mortal! Dost thou think it a slight honour to touch this pipe? Orpheus borrowed it. The Bacchanals heard the same on Mount Cithairon [Cithaeron]. It has never changed; it will never change. The singer passes away; the song remains. Your poets have stolen it in the hush of midnight or of noon. But it is not vouchsafed to all, and lest the few betray us – lest the few betray us, we intoxicate them, we madden them, and so the world cannot believe or understand. Those who have once heard it may be sad or joyous, but their sadness is not the world's, nor their joy; there is ever-more a joy in their sorrow, a sorrow in their joy; they will weep at the bridal, at the burial laugh. But none ever touched these reeds, and thou rejectest them.'

'Thou hast,' the youth answered fearfully, 'made me hate men with thy song. How joyous I yet could be if other men were my only foes!'

'Foolish one!' cried the god. 'What matters it – to lose men – if thou couldst share in the workings of the young year, be one with spring? Deep in the forest, enthroned immortally, sits a godlike woman —.' Pan had laid his hand upon the pipe that hung down in the youth's reluctant grasp, and throwing his head forward, with flashing eyes, until nothing but they and the horns could have been seen by his disciple, 'Aye! but raise not expectant eyes,' he continued, as the listener was about to interrupt, 'not even the gods have often seen her. We know only her thresholds. Around that throne is peace, whom thou knowest not – peace, where hardly the seasons bring change, where the years roll in vain, vain, at least, for harm. The very trees have voices of comfort. "Rest, rest, perturbed earth," is their cry. Her, too, thou mightest know. And consider what empire over the hearts of men thy new wisdom must give thee.'

'Power I covet not,' said the youth.

'If thou shouldst still desire what the world desires, that also thou shouldst have in plenty,' Pan went on. 'Your magicians dreamed of making gold from leaves. I know,

I can tell thee, the mystery of the buttercup's gold –
palpable sunshine; mere earth become matter almost
spiritual.'

'I will not have it,' murmured the youth. 'Alas! how
melancholy the chill coming on of night! I fear to-mor-
row's dawn. I will not play.'

'Unwise! but think of thy skill in love, having this lore,'
insinuated Pan.

'I will not.'

'Thou couldst enjoy the liberties of earth and air and
sea and things thou dreamst not of.'

'I will not.'

'Thou couldst make men wiser –.'

The youth raised the pipe and began to play. First, he
essayed a rural tune, from which he circled upward in
widening sweep, as of eagles climbing, through love,
ambition, grief, joy, and still upward to an utterance of the
deep fears and hopes of men. One sound was a tone as
of souls looking back with earth-memories while passing
the gate of the unknown. Yet the song was puissant rather
in aspiration than achievement; and when he ceased, the
singer wept at the thought of what the song might have
been, crying at last, 'Let me try once again!' That was
unnecessary. Pan had already capitulated. He took the
youth by the hand, entrusting him even with the pipe.
Deeper and deeper into the forest they went. In the after-
noon a gauzy moon had scaled cloud after cloud of the
pallid east; now for a moment a sole tender star throbbed
in that one placid space of milky blue amid the tumul-
tuous cloud; and at length, in the quiet evening, with a few
planets in the blanched blue, and a transparent golden
silk drawn across the west, the gloomy, tranquil cattle
were noisily ruminating in a white mist over the grass. Far
away, sunny cones of wheat still glimmered on the hills.

Boughs made no sound as these two passed – seemed, in fact, to yield like the arms of a sleeper when we alter their place. Now and then they halted, while Pan taught the secrets of the earth, the value of this and that blossom or stem. The fingers of the god shook like a child's as he offered the plants in turn. 'This,' he explained at last, with a languid purple flower in his hand, 'blesses the eater with eternal bliss of sleep'.

They went on, both alarmed whenever night loosened a leaf or two from the forest roof, and at the lights glancing overhead in the green clerestory of the wood, when Pan presently missed his companion. He had noticed the youth loitering somewhat, as if anxious to learn more, and now saw him sinking to the ground. On reaching the spot, a deep sleep already claimed him; the purple petals lay over his cheeks like blood. 'Foolish one!' sighed Pan, 'he sleeps, and will never wake. As for me, I will wait no longer.' Tenderly he folded the youth's white fingers across his breast, wiped the crimson lips, took away the seven-reeded pipe and began to play. Slowly, earnestly, like one making a testament, while death is still out of sight but not out of thought, he brought once again to light all the famous memories of his old life, by means of that music which was of all the most renowned. He recalled how, in hiding among the cattle at Bethlehem, he had witnessed the Nativity, with its cordon of venerable bystanders. He had been a wanderer. He had followed the chase, and his huntsmen had been those spirits of the dead who make the echo; in Wales it had been called 'Arthur's' hunting. The moist eyes flashed again at the thought of his gamesome tasting of the mere odours of the sacrifice, before the pious worshippers had gone and he could press his teeth into it! Now, however, the vanity of all that seemed great; he would never repeat it. He could command adoration from none: it was time to be gone. Never again should strange ardours riot in his frame after a draught of the crimson hedgerow vintages. Mortals should now take an overflowing measure of revenge for the death of Marsyas at Apollo's hands.

He rose, therefore, and took the seven-reeded pipe, and buried it, whence none – perhaps – might ever disinter it; then returned, and took his place beside the youth, where he also entered an eternal sleep. (*Horae Solitariae*, 64–85)

Music – No Man's Garden,

'England is not such a place as it was when I was a young man. It is not half the size for one thing. Why, when I was a young man, you could go up a lane with a long dog or two and pick up a bit of supper and firing and nothing said. The country seemed to belong to me in those days, but now I might as well be in Africa. I am worse off than the labourers now, except that I have got more sense than they have, singing their silly old songs, like this. Then he sang with perhaps mock sentimentality a frail little peasant song, full of the smallness of lonely, small lives: –

> Mary come into the field
> To work along of I,
> Digging up mangold wurzels,
> For they be a-growing high.
> > Dig 'em up by the roots,
> > Dig 'em up by the roots,
> > Put in your spade,
> > Don't be afraid,
> > Dig 'em up by the roots.

Our master is a hard one.
He pays us very small;
And if we stop a moment
We hear his voice to call –
    'Dig 'em up by the roots,' etc.

We work all day together,
Till all the light is past;
And only going homewards
Do we join hands at last.
    'Dig 'em up by the roots,' etc.

For many years we've been sweethearts
And worked the fields along.
And sometimes even now
Mary will sing the old song –
    'Dig 'em up by the roots,' etc.

'What is that to the song about "the swift and silly doe" my old father used to sing to us, or about "Gentle Jenny" the mare that threw the fellow that wasn't going to pay for her hire. No, there is no room in England now for toe-rags like me and you; if you wanted to, you couldn't sleep on Bearsted Green to-night.' (From 'No Man's Garden', *The Heart of England*, 36–7)

'An Old Song' (December 1914, *Last Poems*)

I was not apprenticed nor ever dwelt in famous
    Lincolnshire;
I've served one master ill and well much more than
    seven year;
And never took up to poaching as you shall quickly
    find;
    But 'tis my delight of a shiny night in the season
    of the year.

I roamed where nobody had a right but keepers and
    squires, and there
I sought for nests, wild flowers, oak sticks, and
    moles, both far and near.
And had to run from farmers, and learnt the Lincoln-
    shire song:
    'Oh, 'tis my delight of a shiny night in the season
    of the year.'

I took those walks years after, talking with friend or
    dear,
Or solitary musing; but when the moon shone clear
I had no joy or sorrow that could not be expressed
    By ''Tis my delight of a shiny night in the season
    of the year.'

Since then I've thrown away a chance to fight a
    gamekeeper;
And I less often trespass, and what I see or hear
Is mostly from the road or path by day: yet still I sing:
    'Oh, 'tis my delight of a shiny night in the season
    of the year.'

For if I am contented, at home or anywhere,
Or if I sigh for I know not what, or my heart beats
    with some fear,
It is a strange kind of delight to sing or whistle just:
    'Oh, 'tis my delight of a shiny night in the season
    of the year.'

And with this melody on my lips and no one by to
    care,
Indoors, or out on shiny nights or dark in open air,

I am for a moment made a man that sings out of
    his heart:
    'Oh, 'tis my delight of a shiny night in the season
    of the year.'

44 Virgil, *Georgics* 11 – 'Rivers beneath those ancient walls'.

45 Source unknown.

46 The source for this quote (and p ossibly also the story) is *Obser-vations on the Snowdon Mountains* by William Williams, published in London in 1802.

47 William Blake, 'To the Christians', from *Jerusalem: The Emanation of the Giant Albion* (1804).

48 Thomas quotes from *Lectures on the manuscript materials of ancient Irish history:* delivered at the Catholic University of Ireland, during the sessions of 1855 and 1856, by Eugene O'Curry (Dublin: William A. Hinch, 1861) p. 282.

Acknowledgements

A particular group of people have made this book possible – you know who you are.

I would like to thank Peter Garner, the Friends of the Dymock Poets, especially Richard Simkin, Barbara Davis and Roger Ebbatson, the Edward Thomas Fellowship and the Edward Thomas Literary Estate for their support with the PhD project that began my research on Edward Thomas.

I dedicate this book to the memory of my grandmother, Joan Stenning (née Doe), a child of the South Downs who loved wild flowers, and who died in March 2016.

Anna Stenning;   March 2017

Bibliography

Edward Thomas, 1897. *The Woodland Life* (London: W. Blackwood).
1902. *Horae Solitariae* (London: Duckworth; edition used New York: Dutton)
1903. *Rose Acre Papers* (London: Brown Langham & Co; this edition, London: Duckworth,   1910 – updated)
1903. *Oxford* (London: A. & C. Black).
1905. *Beautiful Wales* (London: A. & C. Black).
1906. *The Heart of England* (London: Dent).
1907. 'Introduction', in *British Country Life in Summer and Spring – The Book of the Open Air*, edited by Edward Thomas (London: Hodder and Stoughton).
1907. 'Introduction', in *The Pocket Book of Poems and Songs for the Open Air, 1907*, edited by Edward Thomas (London: E. Grant Richards).
1909. *Richard Jefferies; His Life and His Work* (London: Hutchinson).
1909. *The South Country* (London: Dent).
1910. *Rest and Unrest* (London: Duckworth).
1911. *Celtic Stories* (Oxford: Clarendon Press).
1911. *Light and Twilight* (London: Duckworth).
1913. *The Icknield Way* (London: Constable).
1913. *The Country* (London: Batsford).
1913. *The Happy-Go-Lucky Morgans* (London: Duckworth).
1914. *In Pursuit of Spring* (London: Thomas Nelson and Sons).
(1915) 2001. *Four-and-Twenty Blackbirds* (London: Duckworth; 2001 reprint by Cheltenham: The Cyder Press).
('Edward Eastaway'), 1917. *Poems* (London: Selwyn & Blount(
1917. *A Literary Pilgrim in England* (London: Methuen).
1918. *Last Poems* (London: Selwyn & Blount).
(1928) 1972. *The Last Sheaf* (London: Jonathan Cape – this edition Freeport, New York: Essay. Index Reprint Series 1972).
1968. *Letters from Edward Thomas to Gordon Bottomley*, edited and introduced by R. George Thomas (London: OUP).

Archive:
The War Diary, unpublished notebook 1917. Hard copy in National Library of Wales, Thomas Family Private Collection. This edition draws on the University of Oxford's First World War Poetry Digital Archive: http://ww1lit.nsms.ox.ac.uk/ww1lit/collections/document/1693

A full bibliography, including secondary sources, can be accessed at www.galileopublishing.co.uk/